Essays on Beauty and the Arts

Bernard Bolzano

Essays on Beauty and the Arts

Bernard Bolzano

Edited by Dominic McIver Lopes
Translated by Adam Bresnahan

Hackett Publishing Company, Inc.
Indianapolis/Cambridge

For further information, please address
        Hackett Publishing Company, Inc.
        P.O. Box 44937
        Indianapolis, Indiana 46244-0937

        www.hackettpublishing.com

Cover design by Listenberger Design & Associates
Interior design by Laura Clark
Composition by Aptara, Inc.

Library of Congress Control Number: 2022938681

ISBN-13: 978-1-64792-091-3 (pbk.)
ISBN-13: 978-1-64792-102-6 (PDF ebook)

The paper used in this publication meets the minimum requirements of
American National Standard for Information Sciences—Permanence of
Paper for Printed Library Materials, ANSI Z39.48–1984.

∞

To James Shelley and Rachel Zuckert

Contents

List of Illustrations

PREFACE

My favorite passage from Bernard Bolzano's writings in aesthetics appears toward the end of the essay on the arts, where he has taken up works that conjoin music with visual art. He remarks, "When children and young people hear cheerful music, do they not feel almost compelled to make a dancing movement and thus to create a visual work of art that changes as we watch? In this case, the musical artwork calls forth the visual artwork without further effort" (§38). That a child, moving to the groove, is the example that comes first to Bolzano's mind beautifully captures the spirit of his work, touching on why he ought to be on everyone's aesthetics must-read list.

Bolzano was born in 1781. His father had moved at an early age from Italy to Prague, where he was an art dealer. The household was severe: "the goddess of affection was banished forever... and in her place there ruled with an iron rod cold, commercial worry for the future and the strict observance of old house rules" (quoted in Rusnock and Šebestík 2019: 23). His parents set examples of "indefatigable" work, and Bolzano recalled, with a hint of regret, how he had to learn from second-hand descriptions what it was like to take a break. The work ethic was to pay dividends—Bolzano's collected writings now run to a hundred volumes—and he was an industrious student at Charles University in Prague. Enrolled in philosophy, he was won over by a reading of Abraham Kästner's *Foundations of Mathematics* to the overlap between mathematics and philosophy. He admired that Kästner took the trouble to prove what is passed over as already familiar: "he attempted to make clear to the reader the reasons upon which his judgment rested—this I liked the best of all" (quoted in Rusnock and Šebestík 2019: 27–28). It was to be a model for his own writing.

Yet Bolzano never wished for the life of the scholar engaged in abstruse meditations for their own sake. Despite his father's urging him to carry on the family business, he grappled from an early age with how he might best serve the common good. For a person of his background, the priesthood was an appealing option, because the church provided education, medical care, and shelter for the indigent and infirm, performing functions of what we would now call an NGO. Although he was skeptical about the creed and spoke out against church abuse of power, Bolzano settled upon the view that religious belief is justified pragmatically. He would also have been aware that members of the clergy had more freedom of expression than the laity, albeit not much, by absolute measures, in the Habsburg Empire under Franz I.

Having been ordained, Bolzano was appointed professor of religion in 1805 and charged with delivering sermons and lectures on the "principles of Christian morality" to all undergraduates at Charles University. The newly created "Catechist" chair was part of a campaign on the part of Franz's reactionary administration to roll back the social reforms that had been introduced by Joseph II in the second half of the eighteenth century. The student body resented church and state control of the curriculum and attended Bolzano's inaugural lecture intending to drown him out with desk thumping, a form of applause (deplatforming is not a new thing). However, Bolzano was firmly on the side of building upon Joseph II's social reforms, and he had the courage to use what latitude he had to speak freely. He ended up charming his audience (Lapointe 2011: 2). Surviving the university's attempt to fire him a few months later, he continued to press for social reform as what we would now call a "politically engaged public intellectual," winning large audiences drawn from both town and gown.

Two features of Bolzano's reform agenda deserve attention.

For a start, Bolzano did not concoct abstract, utopian, or revolutionary schemes. Quite apart from the steady state injustice of social arrangements in early modern Europe, violent conflict laid much of the continent to waste with grim regularity throughout Bolzano's lifetime. He wrote that

> The frequent wars conducted with unprecedented brutality that swept over Europe from one end to the other have visited on us innumerable evils of all kinds. For centuries there have not been as many unfortunates who were robbed of their property, of their limbs, who crawl about gruesomely mutilated; there have not been as many mothers and

fathers who mourn a beloved son who was to be their support in old age; or children who cry for their father and supporter. (quoted in Rusnock and Šebestík 2019: 24)

Violent revolution only made the poor worse off, and Bolzano was acutely aware of the impact on his own upbringing of the pervasive and justified fear of impending ruin that afflicted middle-class families. As a result, the reforms he pushed were targeted and incremental, exactly the ones that were implemented over the next two centuries (see Bolzano 2007). He championed a social safety net: schooling for all children, including health and sex education; free access to university, public libraries, and museums; universal health care; and parks with hiking trails. He also championed political rights: the vote for women and measures to protect Bohemia's ethnic and linguistic diversity. In his vision of social reform, Bolzano is closer to figures such as Jeremy Bentham and John Stuart Mill than to his German contemporaries.

Added to this, Bolzano is an enlightenment reformer, with a twist. Social progress is fueled by knowledge and a respect for the facts. He recommended

> the appropriate development of the power of judgment in each individual citizen, as well as a certain stock of useful knowledge, especially healthy, correct concepts of everything having to do with virtue and happiness, attention directed toward the common best, direction and instruction in correctly judging whether something is beneficial or harmful for the common best, knowledge of the rights a people possess, and the ability to tell the difference between wise and unwise measures. (quoted in Rusnock and Šebestík 2019: 127)

The twist is that Bolzano sees enlightenment as more than what it takes to think for oneself; enlightenment is a social project. In an Easter sermon on enlightenment, he advises that we are "never to look upon the wisdom of other people as a threat" (Bolzano 2007: 58). Indeed, as Paul Rusnock and Jan Šebestík explain, he thought that the most important truths "enjoin various forms of cooperation among the members of a society, and are thus impotent unless they are shared" (2019: 128).

By 1818, the Austrian authorities had had enough. Bolzano was denounced as "the chief pseudo-prophet of our age" (quoted in Rusnock and Šebestík 2019: xxxii), and the following year he was suspended from teaching and publishing, pending an investigation for heresy. He was eventually acquitted, but the gag order remained in place for some time. Supported by his friend Anna Hoffman and her husband, he used the newfound time to write his most important work, including the aesthetics, completed just before his death in 1848.

The standard story of Bolzano's reception makes a pair of complementary moves.

Step one stresses how much Bolzano goes against the grain of nineteenth-century German-language philosophy. He was himself aware of his being out of place. He regarded Immanuel Kant as having derailed philosophy by replacing thinking about the world with thinking about thought about the world, and much of his own work endeavors to undo this error. A page-long footnote to the essay on beauty contains an exasperated tirade against "speculation" in G. W. F. Hegel, and in the essay on the arts he painfully admits that he writes "much too straightforwardly to satisfy the taste *of our time*" (§6). On every front—substantive, methodological, and stylistic—he is out of step with post-Kantian German philosophy (see the Appendix below). His work was pretty much forgotten, but because of his social advocacy, he was soon made and still remains a Czech hero.

Step two tells the story of his gradual discovery as a precursor to contemporary analytic philosophy. Alexius Meinong and Edmund Husserl absorb his work, Alfred Tarski and W. V. O. Quine credit his accounts of logical consequence and logical truth, and scholars give him the nod for anticipating key ideas in Gottlob Frege, including the anti-psychologism and the sense-reference distinction (e.g., Dummett 1991: vii). Indeed, Bolzano's influence on Husserl is arguably an early bridge between analytic philosophy and phenomenology (Lapointe 2011: ch. 11).

As accurate and exciting as this narrative may be, Bolzano's work is enriched by reading it in light of his commitment to social betterment, especially as that commitment is refracted by his modesty, empathy, power of observation, and trust in communicability as a basis for shared understanding. As a case in point, Bolzano's magnum opus, the *Theory of Science* (2014[1837]), closes with a meticulous discussion of how to communicate what we know so as to maximize its social benefits. (Alas, science still struggles to shape public policy.) Given his thoughtful guidance on how to organize writing and how to use language and illustrations to convey ideas, Bolzano's late interest in aesthetics is no surprise.

So, even as the standard story applies to Bolzano's aesthetics, we should also read him for his vision of aesthetic activity as an engine of social progress.

Bolzano is not well known among philosophers working in aesthetics. In 1981, Peter McCormick penned the first study of the beauty essay in English, making a point of Bolzano's "extraordinarily persistent concern for conceptual clarity, argumentative thoroughness, and systematic development" (1981: 107). In her 2006 survey of Austrian aesthetics, Maria Reicher dubbed Bolzano a "forerunner of analytic aesthetics" (2006: 294). Yet the beauty essay did not appear in English until 2015, and the essay on the arts is translated for the first time here (French translations of both appeared in 2017). Paisley Livingston's 2014, 2015, and 2016 articles carefully step through the arguments and supply excellent conceptual background. Bolzano scholars have taken notice: Rusnock and Šebestík's book, *Bolzano, His Life and Work,* concludes with a chapter on the aesthetics, reviewing some short, early writings and providing a comprehensive summary of the second, historical half of the beauty essay, not translated here (2019: 570–78). Nevertheless, there is no entry on Bolzano among the 815 articles that comprise the second edition of the *Oxford Encyclopedia of Aesthetics* (Kelley 2014), and he is not once mentioned in Paul Guyer's (2014) monumental, three-volume *History of Modern Aesthetics.*

In his concerns and in the styles of reasoning he brings to bear on those concerns, Bolzano is far closer to the mainstream of contemporary aesthetics than any philosopher of the eighteenth or nineteenth centuries, equaling Johann Gottfried Herder, especially as interpreted by Rachel Zuckert (2019). In writing about beauty and the arts, he eschews grandiose schemes, takes care not to dwell on outlier cases, and always hews close to the empirical reality of human action and cognition. Beauty and the arts are sites of engagement for everyone, from the dancing child to the artist who composed the music she dances to. Seeing this, Bolzano sets out to illuminate what it is to be beautiful and what it is for any activity to aim at the beautiful. The form of his theories is immediately familiar to us now, and their content is largely revealed in the arguments he gives. These he sets out more explicitly than is often achieved even today, ordering them in his exposition according to their form—arguments from extensional adequacy, inferences to the best explanation, and tenability arguments all do their part.

Livingston correctly points out that Bolzano anticipates the processing fluency theory of beauty proposed by the psychologist Rolf Reber and his collaborators (Livingston 2014: 281–82; e.g., Reber, Schwarz, and Winkielman 2004). In general, Bolzano would have found himself at home in the atmosphere of cognitivism and openness to psychology that has pervaded mainstream aesthetics since the 1960s. More particularly, he anticipates Mohan Matthen (2020) on aesthetic culture, Robert Hopkins (1998) on depiction, and Lopes (2014) on art media.

That Bolzano might resonate for us now is no small matter. The history of analytic aesthetics is dominated by writing on Kant and, to a lesser extent, David Hume. Both influenced subsequent thinking, and both have their partisans nowadays, but the views of neither appeal to your average philosopher working in the field. We badly need to excavate alternatives to the tradition of Hume and Kant. The dig is under way (e.g., Baumgartner and Pasquerella 2006, Copenhaver 2015, Lopes 2019, Zuckert 2019, Matherne 2020, Buchenau 2021, Whiting 2022). Bolzano is the kind of find who ought to motivate more exploration. Influence is not everything, and we should not let his having been overlooked be a reason to leave Bolzano on ice.

Above all, Bolzano has something new to tell us about aesthetics. To fully appreciate his message, we should look out for the role that beauty and the arts can play in the long struggle for a better future for us all. A key to social reform, for Bolzano, is learning, especially shared learning, and it turns out that learning is more intimately tied to beauty and the arts than appears at first.

Consider Bolzano's dancing child one last time. She does not merely dance along with the music. Her dancing along with the music constitutes, for Bolzano, a work of visual art—a work of the kind that a theory of visual art had better shed light on. We must make sense of her as an artist alongside the artist who composed the music she dances to. The difference between them is just the obvious one, a difference in learning. As Bolzano will explain, beauty and the arts are symptoms of learning. A society where there is social improvement through enlightenment is one where beauty and the arts will thrive.

DML
Vancouver, Canada
March 2022

Translation Notes
and Glossary

A version of the translation of "On the Concept of the Beautiful" was first published in *Estetika: The European Journal of Aesthetics* 52.2 (2015): 229–66. Stylistic changes have been made to that text, most notably in applying a policy on gendered language (see below), and some technical terms have been edited to match the glossary (also below). Beyond that, the translation has been edited throughout with an eye to the integrity of the essay's philosophical content. For reasons of space, the historical overview in §§26–57 is not included. The source text is Bernard Bolzano, *Über den Begriff des Schönen* (Prague: Borrosch et André, 1843).

The source text for "On the Classification of the Fine Arts" is Bernard Bolzano, *Über die Einteilung der schönen Künste* (Prague: Borrosch et André, 1849). Section 40, which displays Bolzano's classification as a list, is excluded. Adam Bresnahan's initial translation has also been edited with an eye to the integrity of the essay's philosophical content.

Explanatory interpolations and editorial footnotes are in [square brackets].

Language that is genderless in German has been put into genderless English, sometimes taking advantage of the singular "they." However, assumptions about gender that would have been commonplace among Bolzano's peers have been retained. For example, "he" and "him" are used as pronouns for "artist."

Technical terms have been translated as shown in the following word list, which largely follows the pattern of recent Bolzano translations. A notable exception is the translation of "*Erklärung*" as "explication," for reasons given in the Introduction. English terms shown in parentheses in the glossary are those used in the *Estetika* translation but deprecated in this volume.

Bolzano uses several German words for hedonic states. *"Vergnügen"* and *"Wohlgefallen"* have been translated as "pleasure" since they appear most frequently and are used to denote hedonic response quite broadly. *"Angenehme"* appears on about twenty occasions, almost always when the topic is sensory pleasure; it is rendered as "gratification." *"Genuss"* and *"Lust"* are rare and are used for emphasis; they are translated as "enjoyment" and "delight."

Although *"Bildung"* can be put into English as "education," the German is broader and does not connote formal schooling. Better translations are "formation" or "development." When "development" does not work on its own, the text qualifies the development as cognitive. For Bolzano, facility with concepts is principally a product of natural and informal processes of learning, as §25 of the beauty essay makes especially clear.

Relatedly, *"Anleitung"* is often put into English as "instructions," but an alternative translation is "guidance." In §4 of the essay on the arts, Bolzano contends that artists and others need *Anleitung,* but he also warns that *Anleitung* is not "mere rules and written prescriptions." This is confirmed in book 5 of the *Theory of Science,* where Bolzano provides rich and nuanced advice on presenting what we know. "Guidance" comes closer to Bolzano's meaning than does "instructions."

Two words that can be translated as "poetry" appear in the essays on the fine arts. One is *"Dichtung,"* often paired with *"Gedicht"* for "poem." The other is *"Poesie,"* which Bolzano uses in a way that taps the meaning of the Greek ποίησις, "making." A definition is given in §38 of the essay on the fine arts: *Poesie* is what prompts the imagination to have thoughts without regard to their truth. To capture this, *"Poesie"* has been translated as "inventiveness."

Three terms in the list below have variant translations in special contexts. *"Unmittelbar"* and *"mittelbar"* are normally given as "immediate" and "mediated" but as "direct" and "indirect" when they appear in Bolzano's technical account of the connections between arts. *"Anschauung"* is translated as "awareness" when it is a synonym for *"Bewusstsein,"* or "consciousness," and as "intuition" when Bolzano uses it in its technical sense to denote a representation that has a simple content and a singular extension—notably, a subjective representation caused by our interaction with the world. (See the Introduction for an explanation of this apparatus.)

Drawing the distinction between awareness and intuition requires a decision about how to translate *"Anschauung"* as it appears in Bolzano's theory of beauty. On that theory, apprehending an item's beauty involves an obscure awareness (*Anschauung*) of the proficiency of one's cognitive powers in apprehending the item. Arguably, the awareness is not an intuition. In §280 of the *Theory of Science,* Bolzano takes an obscure intuition to be one of which we do not have another intuition that represents it. Nothing in his account commits him to holding that our awareness of the proficiency of our cognitive powers in the experience of beauty must be obscure in this one sense. The awareness might well be an obscure representation that is not an intuition but rather a concept or a mixed representation. For this reason, *"Anschauung"* is rendered as "awareness" in Bolzano's theory of beauty.

Abhandlung	essay	(treatise)
Angenehme	gratification	(agreeable)
Anleitung	guidance	
Anschauung	awareness/intuition	
Begriff	concept	
Bestandteil	constituent	
Betrachtung	contemplation	
Bewusstsein	consciousness	
Bildung	development	(education)
Dichtkunst	literary art, poetry	
dunkel	obscure	
Empfindung	sensation, rarely feeling	
Erkenntnis	cognition, knowledge	
Erklärung	explication	(definition)
gebunden	constrained	
Gefühl	feeling	(emotion, feeling)
Genuss	enjoyment	
Kraft	power	(faculty)
Lehrbuch	treatise	(textbook)
Lehre	theory	(doctrine)
Lust	delight	

Mensch	human being	(man)
mittelbar	mediated/indirect	
Poesie	inventiveness	
reizend	charming	
Satz	proposition	
Seele	mind	
ungebunden	unconstrained	
unmittelbar	immediate/direct	
Vergnügen	pleasure	(gratification)
Vorstellung	representation	(idea)
Wohlgefallen	pleasure	
Zweck	purpose	

Note for Instructors

In the balance they strike between challenge and accessibility, Bolzano's essays in aesthetics are a treat to teach. Each offers an original and indeed revisionary theory of a phenomenon. Moreover, Bolzano takes his own advice in the *Theory of Science* (2014[1837]) about how to communicate. His no-nonsense prose gets out of the reader's way. Technicalities are avoided where possible. Examples are familiar to all. Key formulations are set in italics, and different types of argument are presented each in its own place. In addition to all of this, however, the essays achieve another kind of accessibility (and challenge), because they are well suited for use in a range of philosophy courses—on Bolzano, the history of early analytic philosophy, philosophy of education, the history of aesthetics, and contemporary aesthetics with a focus on aesthetic value or art or the individual arts.

Before turning to that, some guidance applies to any undergraduate course.

The beauty essay opens with a lengthy discussion of ontology and methodology that is far more technical than the remainder of the essay. Moreover, students with some background in contemporary philosophy will likely take for granted what Bolzano is urging his contemporaries to accept. With exceptions noted below, students might start with the first paragraph of §1 and then jump to §2. The rest of §1 could be skipped altogether, or §1.4 could be read alongside §§11–15.

In portioning out the reading, the text carves at the following joints. General reflections that motivate Bolzano's theory of beauty are laid out in §§2–10, then §§11–15 articulate the theory and argue that it fits our intuitions. In §§16–18 Bolzano defends the theory as best explaining certain facts, and in §§19–25 he replies to objections. All this can be covered in three one-hour lectures.

The essay on the fine arts begins with §§1–10, which lay out a principled framework for thinking about the arts. The framework is used to treat the arts of pure thought in §§11–17, the sonic arts in §§18–27, the visual arts in §18 and §§28–33, and some hybrid arts in §§34–39. Except in courses with a focus on the individual arts, there is little to be lost by assigning either the sonic or the visual arts. Assigning either conveys Bolzano's method in thinking through the theory of an art. If time is an issue, the first ten sections can be taught in an hour's lecture and their application in a second lecture.

Turning to specific courses, it goes without saying that the aesthetics can enrich a course devoted to Bolzano. Taught alongside his writings in ethics, politics, and religion, it displays the scope of his thought. Unlike those writings, however, the aesthetics postdates and integrates the lessons of the *Theory of Science*. The essay on the fine arts is a meta-theory for a collection of sciences—the sciences of the various arts. Meanwhile, the theory of beauty is a lucid example of Bolzano-style explication, and the beauty essay is the place where Bolzano grapples with how we come to form concepts, especially very complex ones, without being aware of their parts (Rusnock and Šebestík 2019: 556). Compact and succinct as they are, one might even read the essays in aesthetics before getting into the weeds in the *Theory of Science*.

Broadening out, Bolzano's aesthetics would make a fresh addition to a course in the history of early analytic philosophy. By including aesthetics, it would diversify the range of topics covered. More importantly, the theory of beauty is a rich and self-contained instance of what was sought by later philosophers under the rubric of analysis, explication, or clarification. As a bonus, Bolzano is exceptionally explicit about the role of counterexamples and objections in testing his theory, and his remarks about concept formation, mentioned in the previous paragraph, also address the paradox of analysis. For this course and for a course dedicated just to Bolzano, §1 of the beauty essay should be read in full.

Bolzano deserves more attention as a philosopher of education. Inasmuch as he argues that art is something that can be taught and that is crucial for teaching anything else, the essays can make a distinctive contribution to the philosophy of art education. A fruitful angle would explore the matched emphasis on learning in the essay on beauty and on guidance in the essay on the arts. In matching guidance to learning, Bolzano also ties aesthetics to science and to social betterment.

He would have endorsed the agenda of Nelson Goodman and Project Zero.

Whether there is room for Bolzano in a course in the history of aesthetics very much depends on how the course is conceived. Standardly conceived, Immanuel Kant marks the end of the line for approaches that foreground beauty and aesthetic judgment. Friedrich Schelling and G. W. F. Hegel foreground art, to be understood as a mode of access to special truths, and they set the agenda for subsequent thinkers through to Theodor Adorno and Arthur Danto. In a course that examines how each figure responds to their predecessors in the canon, Bolzano might have little to offer. Viewed in contrast to the post-Kantians, he seems too close to Kant. That is the case against. The case in favor is that Bolzano's aesthetics stands out, historically, as a vigorous attempt to counter post-Kantian trends. Reading Bolzano from this angle requires careful attention to how much, appearances aside, he disagrees with Kant. Bolzano's is an approach to beauty and the arts without disinterested, nonconceptual, universal, and necessary pleasure, also without free play and genius. An Appendix to the Introduction details the relationship between Bolzano and Kant and teases out what their differences tell us about Bolzano's critique of Kant's successors.

Many aesthetics courses are organized around contemporary work on a suite of topics. Instructors who would like to kick off with a serving of history face a conundrum about what to assign. Kant is far too demanding in a number of respects. For other writers, we have a choice of unsystematic essays or excerpts from longer texts, many not written by philosophers. The result has been a relative absence of history from aesthetics courses. Perhaps Bolzano can do for aesthetics what Mill and Kant do for ethics. His essays in aesthetics can be used to launch a course that goes on to highlight the usual suspects among contemporary writers on theories of art and the aesthetic. Even better, no historical source beats Bolzano's second essay as an anchor for a course focused on the individual arts. That essay is provocatively systematic. Refusing to defer to what everyone counts as art, he proceeds instead on a principled basis, with the result that he foresees what have turned out to be important new art forms.

Provocations motivate learning, and Bolzano obliges. Perfect intellects cannot take pleasure in beauty. Philosophy and the sciences are arts. Bolzano anticipates so much late twentieth-century art: Why was he alone in this? What would he have thought about video games and the arts of agency? No doubt you and your students will add to the list as you read.

ACKNOWLEDGMENTS

Those who know me will share my surprise at having taken on an edition of two nineteenth-century texts. The project only got off the ground with encouragement and support from members of the community of Bolzano scholars. Sandra Lapointe, to whom I first broached the idea, assured me that I was onto something worthwhile and gave me some choice names to contact, some of whom supplied further names. Paisley Livingston, who has led the way in introducing Bolzano to anglophone aesthetics, warmly encouraged my efforts, corrected my errors, pushed for an improved translation of the explication of aesthetics, and gifted me with an elegant way to handle the distinction between the arts and the fine arts. Clinton Tolley held my feet to the fire on nuances of translation and pressed me to articulate how Bolzano goes beyond Kant. Carole Maigné green-lighted some of my readings and proposed an extremely interesting alternative reading of the theory of beauty that I hope to discuss elsewhere. I have learned that the world of Bolzano is generous and kind to visitors.

Markus Hallensleben kindly advised on note 18 of the beauty essay, Sandra Lapointe helped with note 18 of the essay on the arts, and Whitney Davis, Joseph Monteyne, and Paisley Livingston helped with note 21 of the same essay. Members of my third-year course in aesthetics bravely read the first draft, making countless suggestions that boosted its accessibility. My thanks to Rebecca Byle, Jonah Kohn, Cynthia MacMillan, Marilo Marino, Aman Mathur, Rayva Nelson, Aidan Perreault, Dove Uy, and Jiaxin Zhang, in particular.

Not everyone has drunk the Bolzano Kool-Aid. Sympathetic outsiders, Rachel Zuckert and two anonymous referees, articulated insights whose impact pervades the final version. Hande Tuna graciously set me straight on how to sum up Kant in the Appendix. Remarks by Zuckert and one of the referees shook up my thinking about ways to teach Bolzano.

Working with a translator was a learning experience, and Adam Bresnahan made it a joy. See the essay on beauty for what follows from that. My thanks also to the Social Sciences and Humanities Research Council of Canada for a grant that funded the translation of the essay on the arts. A final thanks to Jeff Dean, whose philosophical and editorial acumen makes me all the more grateful for his having taken this volume under his wing.

INTRODUCTION

Bolzano's writings in aesthetics are essays, albeit long ones, and the format is significant. In his great study, *Theory of Science*, Bolzano takes stock of the kinds of texts that we can use to document and communicate what we know. Unlike a *Lehrbuch*, or treatise, which "encompasses the entirety of a science," an essay advances "theses concerning which we have something special to say separately . . . rather than combining them with all the remaining theses of the science" (Bolzano 2014[1837]: §712). True to form, the essays on beauty and the arts tell only part of what we wish to know from the field of aesthetics (Bolzano started but did not complete two more essays; see Bolzano 2021, Livingston 2022). Yet it would be a mistake either to treat the essays on beauty and the arts as freestanding or to treat the essay on the arts as nothing but an application of the theory of beauty. Bolzano's thinking is always systematic: Each essay gives substance to what the other proposes and lends weight to its counterpart's argument. Each unpacks a component of the explication of aesthetics in the first section of the essay on the arts. They must be read together to fully appreciate their context, their content, and their method of reasoning.

Context

Despite his position outside mainstream nineteenth-century aesthetics, Bolzano was not indifferent to the questions to which his peers turned to philosophy for answers. His conception of what it would take to answer them was new, as were the answers he gave, but the essays on beauty and the arts are products of what the French helpfully call the *"problématique"* of his times, a problematic that shaped the formation of the entire discipline of philosophical aesthetics. What follows is a story familiar from the history books (esp. Kristeller 1951–52, Abrams 1989,

1

Shiner 2001; see also Lopes 2014: ch. 2, Wolterstorff 2015: ch. 1). That history ought to be (it rarely is) kept in mind whenever we wonder what we want philosophical accounts of beauty and the arts to be. At any rate, it illuminates the interplay of Bolzano's essays on those topics. In his "sociology of modern aesthetics," the literary scholar M. H. Abrams unmasks a "situation" that we so take for granted in current thinking about the arts that "an effort of historical imagination" is needed to see it for what it is (1989: 22). The situation has two central elements, one detailed by P. O. Kristeller (1951–52) and the other emphasized by Abrams himself. Supplementing the two central elements are a number of further theses and causal hypotheses, many of which are controversial (e.g., Halliwell 2002, Porter 2009, Kivy 2012). We need not dwell on them, for the central elements stand on their own and are widely accepted (Lopes 2014: 27–28, Wolterstorff 2015: 10–11; cf. Young 2015).

Pictures are often good for nudging the imagination along. Figure 1 reproduces a tree diagram from the preface to Ephraim Chambers's *Cyclopaedia* of 1728. The diagram embodies Chambers's view of the most perspicuous and handy division of human knowledge. Look for the arts: you will find them scattered across the tree. Painting branches off optics, music off applied mathematics, and gardening off agriculture, while poetry keeps company with rhetoric, grammar, and . . . heraldry. Chambers inspired Denis Diderot and Jean-Baptiste le Rond d'Alembert's work on their *Encyclopédie* of 1751, which also features a tree of human knowledge (fig. 2). Notice that the arts are now prominent, grouped together with one another and apart from the other main branches of knowledge.

According to Kristeller, the crystallization of a new concept—fine arts—spread across Europe between 1728 and 1751. Such a concept is, at bottom, a disposition to group together some activities or practices and to distinguish them from other activities or practices. Whatever the grouping's precise membership, the fine arts were complements of three other new groupings: the liberal arts or humanities, the practical arts, and the sciences. From our perspective today, little is more obvious than this arrangement. In fact, though, it is an invention of the early modern period.

Figure 1

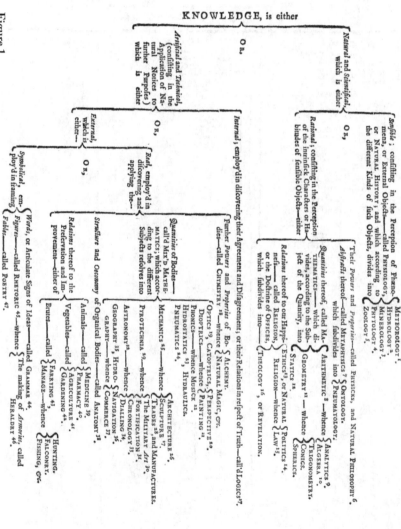

*SYSTÉME FIGURÉ
DES CONNOISSANCES HUMAINES.

ENTENDEMENT.

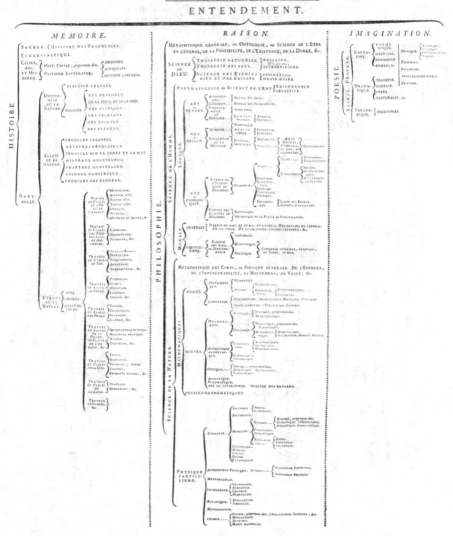

Figure 2

Some caveats. First, the individual arts are obviously not eighteenth-century inventions. Most of them are ancient; indeed, traces of painting, sculpture, and music are to be found in the prehistoric record. As Kristeller puts it, "the various arts are certainly as old as human civilization, but the manner in which we are accustomed to group them . . . is comparatively recent" (1951–52: 45). Second, the crystallization of the concept of the fine arts was not abrupt; it marked the culmination of a gradual process, one that Kristeller chronicles over centuries. Third, the extension of the concept was never settled. At first, the concept included only painting, sculpture, architecture, music, and poetry, but landscape architecture, dance, theater, and prose literature soon jostled for admission to the club, and debates still rage about what activities or practices count as arts: Photography? Video games? Wine? Food?

All that is needed to fill in Bolzano's context is that philosophers had come to see it as one of their tasks to give a theory of the fine arts. The theory would state what features belong to all the arts and only the arts—what they share in common that sets them apart from the liberal arts, applied arts, and sciences. In the eighteenth century, the need for such a theory was called the "problem of the arts." And it is a tough one. After all, if dance is an art but not ice dance, then what is the difference between them? Ditto for novels and biographies, plays and parades, abstract paintings and fireworks. The problem of the arts, which is assumed to be a philosophical problem, is one central element of Abrams's situation.

The second element is one that Kristeller discerns but Abrams characterizes with decided lucidity. Given that the arts antedate the eighteenth century, the problem of the arts nevertheless puts a spin on how we should think about them.

Abrams argues that earlier thought largely took each art on its own terms and only sometimes compared a few arts in limited ways for special purposes. Moreover, each art was understood as a mode of making, "a *techne* or *ars*, that is, a craft, each with its requisite rules for selecting materials and shaping them into a work designed to affect certain external ends" (Abrams 1989: 10). To understand the arts in this way is to view them from the stance of the maker, to adopt a "construction model." On such a model, differences in materials, techniques, and skills highlight the specificities of the arts.

A model that highlights the specificities of the arts serves our purposes, especially when it comes to artistic training, until we confront the problem of the arts. To solve that problem, we identify what the fine arts share in common and come to see their differences principally in light of their commonality. For this reason, Abrams argues, the problem of the arts prompted a shift in stances from that of the maker to that of the receiver, replacing the construction model with a consumption model.

Again, philosophers came to see it as their task to theorize consumption as a phenomenon that cuts across the fine arts and is at the same time unique to them. Of course, people had always, in some sense, consumed works of painting, sculpture, architecture, music, and poetry. They took them in, and they got something from taking them in. Abrams draws a distinction, though. In the earlier period, artworks were typically "produced for a specific function or occasion, religious or secular," and each was experienced as an "integral component in a complex of human activities or functions" (Abrams 1989: 22). Paintings, sculptures, and poems gave instruction, for the most part; works of music and architecture embellished worship and ceremony. All evoked aesthetic experiences as well, but only in the course of serving other purposes. By contrast, in the later period, the assumption was that artworks principally, perhaps exclusively, address an aesthetic interest. "Aesthetic interest" is our phrase. In the eighteenth century, the word was "taste," understood as the personal and psychological underpinnings of appropriate responses to beauty and other aesthetic values.

Joseph Addison hit the nail on the head, as early as 1711, in one of his pieces for *The Spectator*. He remarked that "Musick, Architecture, and Painting, as well as Poetry, and Oratory, are to deduce their Laws and Rules from the general Sense and Taste of Mankind, and not from the Principles of those Arts themselves" (1711). No guidance for creating beauty will be derived from guidance for constructing works of painting, sculpture, architecture, music, or poetry. To understand beauty, we must look at its reception instead. The shift from the construction model to the consumption model takes the focus off the specificities of the individual arts and places it on a "general" taste for beauty that any artwork—that is, a work in any of the fine arts—might address.

Both central elements find concrete embodiment in the rapid emergence of new arts institutions in early modern Europe. The British Museum opened in 1759; the Vatican Museum and the Uffizi in 1773. Great country houses opened their doors to the paying public, who were keen to drink in their landscapes and architecture. The first public concert halls were built. Writers no longer relied on patrons but derived their income from publishers, and the new lending libraries made their wares accessible to the middle classes. Journalistic reviews of salons, books, and concerts offered advice on smart consumption. Indeed, historians propose that economic changes in early modern Europe drove these developments. Taste was at first a monopoly of the gentry, for whom a leisurely pursuit of the arts signaled social status. Soon, members of the new middle classes, finding themselves with spare cash and spare time, further fed the growth of the new art institutions. And what happened in Europe was repeated elsewhere in due course (e.g., in the United States in the late nineteenth century—see Lena 2019). So one side of the coin is that the new institutions position receivers to consume art. The flip side is that the arts are just those activities for which this kind of institutional infrastructure has been built.

A balancing act is needed. Philosophers had shouldered the burden of delivering a theory of the arts plus a theory of beauty (or taste, the response to beauty). The two theories are interdependent. Beauty, whatever it is, must turn out to be what is found above all in the arts. The arts, whatever they are, must turn out to be a preeminent domain of beauty. If the circularity is intolerable, then the challenge is to find a way to make one theory more basic, so that it can be used to ground the other. In retrospect, we know the challenge was formidable. On one hand, each art seems to have so much more in common with some nonarts than with the other arts (dance is more like ice dance than landscape architecture, or even sculpture). On the other hand, if we say that what the arts share in common and what distinguishes them from the nonarts is their appeal to an interest in beauty, then we distort our conception of beauty by downplaying its importance outside the arts—in nature, design, and ideas. The lesson is not that the two elements cannot be reconciled, though that was the conclusion that philosophers did reach in the twentieth century. Rather, acknowledging the size of the challenge helps us to appreciate how radical was Bolzano's approach in his essays on beauty and the arts.

Content: Beauty

Bolzano's deliberations are often so meticulous and studied that their juicy inventiveness is all too easy to miss. Especially forbidding is the official formulation of his theory, or "explication," of beauty. In *Theory of Science*, he gets playfully gnomic: "beauty is suitability recognized obscurely" (2014[1837]: §589). The essay on the concept of beauty is more technical, though, and Bolzano even acknowledges that his explication of beauty can seem "artificial" (§25). Unless tackled head-on, the technicalities can obscure what matters—Bolzano's vision of beauty as diverse, as entangled in practical life, and as a supremely human phenomenon. Unpacking the theory sets us up to spotlight its deep appeal and then sum up the argument.

Here is the official formulation, first stated in §11, twice repeated word for word, and frequently cited throughout the essay:

> the beautiful must be an object whose contemplation can cause pleasure in all people whose cognitive powers are duly developed. This pleasure occurs because, after apprehending some of the object's qualities, the formation of a concept of the object is neither too easy nor too difficult and does not occasion the rigor of distinct thought. Moreover, the pleasure occurs because the concept thus formed, in making it possible to guess at those qualities of the object only accessible to further contemplation, affords at least an obscure awareness of the proficiency of one's cognitive powers.

This explication of the beautiful is couched in terms that would have rung bells in aesthetics—"contemplation," "pleasure," and "self-awareness," in particular. We must not be misled. Bolzano understands these phenomena specifically in the light of his account of cognition.

On holiday in Bali, you are brought to a halt outside a courtyard. A gamelan—an Indigenous orchestra—is performing. Your attention is caught, and you lean in for a closer listen. Listening more closely is contemplating in the sense that you attend to the event in a way that seeks to answer the question, What is this? You try for a concept of it. A concept is a representation of an item's constitutive features that guides your apprehension of other features it is likely to have. A music theorist might arrive at a rigorously technical concept of the work, but you are no music theorist. You get what is happening on a nontechnical level, almost as if you are guessing, but with reliable success. In doing this, you are pleasantly aware of the proficiency of your mind as it makes out the music. You are also pleasantly aware of how your mind has grown more powerful in learning to grapple with something unfamiliar. The music's power to have this effect on you is its beauty.

Start with contemplation. Contemplating the performance is posing a "What is this?" question and then answering it by forming a concept of the performance that leads you to apprehend more of its features. So understood, contemplation is a perfectly ordinary, everyday occurrence. Yet your contemplation contrasts with the music theorist's technical one. Theirs has a rigor of thought that is distinct, hence clear. Yours is not; it is obscure. These are venerable and value-laden metaphors in philosophy: clarity and distinctness are traditionally touted as virtues of cognition . . . not so much obscurity. However, Bolzano does not rely on metaphors; he assigns obscure cognition a paramount role in human life, and he therefore proposes new accounts of clear, distinct, and obscure thought (2014[1837]: §§280–81; see also Krämer 2011, Livingston 2014: 278–81, Livingston 2015: 208–11, Morscher 2018: §§4.1–4.2; a competing interpretation is Vesper 2012).

For Bolzano, some states of mind are either true or false; they are propositional. An example would be your belief that something is a labradoodle. Obviously, thoughts like these are ultimately made up of non-propositional elements; Bolzano calls them "representations." Some representations are concepts, which are complex or general (or both). For example, the concept of labradoodles is general because it covers many items, and it is complex because it is made up of other concepts, such as the concept of dog and the concept of a cross between a poodle and some other breed. Meanwhile, the concept of something is general because it covers many items, but it is not made up of any other concepts, so it is simple rather than complex. Finally, the concept of Lopes's dog is complex but not general (I have only one dog). That leaves representations that are neither complex nor general. Bolzano calls them "intuitions." Intuitions are simple and singular, representing exactly one item. They are expressed by a pure "that" or "this," with no added information. Moreover, Bolzano holds that subjective (i.e., mental) intuitions represent other mental states. A minute ago, you were not thinking about labradoodles, but then the concept of labradoodles came into your mind. Your mind underwent a change. Now you can think about *that*, the change in your mind that occurred a minute ago. The *that* is an intuition of your concept of labradoodles.

Using what Bolzano says about the elements of thought, we can now define clarity with respect to mental concepts. The gamelan performance has a sonic contour, a sequence of sounds with a pitch and a beat. Hearing it, you form a mental concept of it, a concept that equips you to recognize it again and perhaps to hum or clap it back. The concept is complex because it is made up of parts representing the contour's melodic and rhythmic components and how they relate to one another. But remember, not all concepts are complex. Your concept of a piano's middle C might be simple, not made up of parts, but it represents all soundings of middle C. It is general. A mental concept is clear when we represent the concept to ourselves by means of an intuition. To get clarity on your concept of the sonic contour, you have a simple thought, *that*, which is about the change in your mind that is your applying a concept of a sonic contour to what you hear. To get clarity on your concept of middle C, you have a simple thought, *that*, which is about the change in your mind that is your applying the concept of middle C. Clear thought is a kind of self-awareness, or metacognition.

Distinctness is defined in terms of clarity. A mental concept can be distinct in either of two ways. On one hand, your simple concept is distinct just when it is both clear and you have a clear representation of it as simple—as not made up of other concepts. Your simple thought, *that*, represents the concept of middle C as not composed of parts. On the other hand, a complex concept is distinct just when it is clear and you have a clear representation of its parts and how they relate to each other. Either way, a concept's distinctness implies a clear representation of its architecture.

Obscure concepts are, by definition, ones that are not distinct, hence in some respect not clear. As should be obvious, distinct concepts require a degree of self-awareness that is arduous. For scientific and theoretical purposes, the extra work pays off. In the course of everyday life, it does not. I reach for the coffee mug, employing a concept of coffee mugs, without having to go to the trouble of representing to myself the very change in my mind that is my applying a concept of coffee mugs, where I think of the concept as composed of those parts, related as they are. Truth be told, I have no clue of the constituents of my coffee mug concept. That is a good thing. I do not need too much cognition getting between me and my caffeine. In practical life, we manage just fine with obscure concepts; distinct ones are surplus to requirements.

So much for contemplation and self-awareness. How does pleasure come in? Since your contemplation of the gamelan performance does not require a distinct concept of it, you may forego the arduous cognitive labor of the music theorist, who is thinking about every part of their thinking about the music. At the same time, your gamelan encounter is more demanding than mine with the coffee mug: I apply my coffee mug concept to it, but I do not use that concept to apprehend more of its features. It is too early in the day to be contemplating coffee mugs. The gamelan performance is just demanding enough to nudge you to obscurely notice that your mind is busy answering the question, what is this? In §9 Bolzano assumes that we feel pleasure in our awareness of how the exercise of our capacities, including our cognitive capacities, is neither too easy nor too hard. Added to that, we feel pleasure in awareness of the augmentation of our capacities. As you come to terms with the gamelan performance, you feel pleasure in an obscure awareness of flexing and building your mental muscles.

Bolzano advertises these intricacies as needed mainly to secure extensional adequacy—to craft a concept of beauty that applies to all and only beautiful items. Nonetheless, the essay itself, especially §§2–10, gathers up what Bolzano describes as "useful insights" (§6). The intricacies of the explication of the beautiful ultimately speak to them.

First is beauty's entanglement in practical life. Contemplation is not some rarified reverie, nor is it to be equated with the absorbed state of mind encouraged by such settings as concert halls and art galleries. On the contrary, contemplation is the mind performing a perfectly ordinary chore, bringing an item under a concept, with the result that we apprehend more of the item's features. Contemplation can involve distinct concepts, like the music theorist's, or obscure ones, like yours. When it occasions pleasure in beauty, contemplation need only involve the kind of cognition that is suited to practical affairs, where obscure concepts serve perfectly well.

A second and related insight concerns the diversity of the beautiful. Anything is beautiful if it invites us to contemplate what it is, applying obscure concepts, thereby raising to pleasing awareness the growing proficiency of the mind. Works of painting, sculpture, architecture, music, and poetry fit the bill. The logarithmic spiral is a mathematical beauty, and Bolzano would have known that it occurs in nature too (e.g., the nautilus shell in fig. 4). Is there anything in the world that never prompts us to wonder, What is this? And that we can never go on to contemplate in a way that builds mental muscle?

Sections 5 and 6 of the beauty essay further articulate the diversity insight, albeit indirectly. These two sections argue that contemplation in response to beauty does not have any particular content. Bolzano opens §5 with the question, "What aspects of an object do our thoughts engage with such that we experience the beauty of that object?" In other words, can we list the kinds of features that make items beautiful? Philosophers have floated many answers over the centuries. Their suggestions include having a unified diversity of forms, expressing a particularized emotion, or being a perfect instance of its kind. Each of these suggestions restricts what items can be beautiful. For Bolzano, though, pleasure in beauty is "not to be found in the features of the object revealed by our contemplation" (§10).

The third insight is bedrock for Bolzano: beauty is a quintessentially human phenomenon. How Bolzano chooses to express the insight strikes us nowadays as peculiar and borderline offensive. He writes in §10, "A starting point for our inquiry is the fact that only human beings with more or less developed cognitive powers are able to experience this pleasure, animals being wholly incapable of it, higher beings transcending it." Nonhuman animals (and newborn humans) have no eye for beauty at all, divine intelligences know what is beautiful but can take no pleasure in it, and our pleasure in beauty is a function of cognitive development. Superficially, the optics are not good. What we should do as charitable readers is go below the surface. We should rethink the contrasts in the passage from §10 (and similar ones scattered across the essay) as articulating views of the human condition and of beauty as essentially human—views that we would now express in different terms.

To begin with, as commentators invariably remark, the beautiful is response-constituted. Beauty just is a power to produce a specific effect in creatures like us. Yet Bolzano does not make much of the metaphysics (see Livingston 2015: 204–5). Instead, he stresses how beauty reflects the limits and opportunities of human cognition. On one hand, human cognition is self-aware, in the concrete sense that we can and do reflect upon our mental responses to the world. That is the point that matters, though Bolzano makes it by assuming that nonhuman animals and infants lack the same capacity. On the other hand, we are practical creatures: we must make our way in the world, adapting to it and adapting it to us. When Bolzano remarks that we are "born to act rather than to learn," he means that we learn for purposes of acting (2014[1837]: §452). In practical endeavors, obscure concepts serve us well. That is the point that matters, though Bolzano makes it by contrasting us with divine intelligences whose knowledge always transcends that of practical agents such as us. Human pleasure in beauty is a product of both points that matter, which together insist upon the role of obscure thought in our lives.

To unpack the reference to cognitive development, consider Bolzano's ambivalence about the alleged universality of responses to beauty. With a nod to Immanuel Kant, Bolzano writes that "our judgments about beauty make a certain claim to universal validity," and then he adds, "I emphasize, only a *certain* claim to universal validity" (§6). We have just seen that nonhuman animals, infants, and "higher beings" are exceptions, but Bolzano's explication of beauty also predicts intercultural differences. After all, pleasure in beauty accompanies concept acquisition, and we cannot acquire new concepts unless we differ from one another in our conceptual repertoires. And as long as Bolzano's explication allows for cultural variation in conceptual repertoires, it accommodates cultural variation in responses to beauty. Yoking pleasure in beauty to learning naturally explains why aesthetics varies by culture (see Matthen 2020).

In short, Bolzano's explication of beauty hangs upon the details of his account of cognition, but those details unlock a broader vision of human life. His aim is not to establish our exceptionality; it is to portray who we are. We are creatures who find beauty almost everywhere because we are, in our cognitive capacities, creatures whose practical agency is culturally located.

If the picture is attractive, it remains to consider its truth, hence Bolzano's argument in its favor. The first ten sections of the essay develop and state the explication of the concept of beauty. Sections 11–25 set out the arguments with remarkable transparency. In §§16–18, Bolzano presents a suite of abductive arguments: his explication best explains why beauty is often mysterious, why some sense modalities are better suited to apprehending beauty, why beauty tends to go with novelty, why beauty responses are keyed to education, why pleasure in beauty mixes with other pleasures, and why some items are ugly. In §§19–25, Bolzano turns to tenability arguments, which support his explication by answering objections to it. Are there not simple beauties? Beauties that are very easy and very demanding? Irregular ones? Surprising ones? In replying to each concern, Bolzano takes care to point out to his reader precisely what clauses of his explication are at issue.

That leaves §§11–15, where Bolzano makes the case for extensional adequacy. Here, matters get trickier, for Bolzano grants that more items count as beautiful on his explication than we otherwise count as beautiful. In what sense, then, is the explication extensionally adequate? The search for an answer will lead us to the essay on the fine arts, by way of a closer look at his philosophical method.

Method

Sandra Lapointe likens Bolzano's explications to those of Rudolf Carnap. For both, the aim is "making more exact a vague or not quite exact concept used in everyday life or in an earlier stage of scientific or logical development" (2011: 36, quoting Carnap 1947: 7–8). Notice the second disjunction. Concepts are used in everyday life and also in scientific inquiry. Are we to take it that the correct explication of the concept of beauty used in everyday life is never in tension with the one that figures, as Bolzano puts it, in treatises in aesthetics? If they do conflict, which has priority? Bolzano grapples with the problem in a big way in

§1 of the beauty essay, and his solution to it also frames the essay on the fine arts (cf. Rusnock and Šebestík 2019: 533–35).

First, Bolzano distinguishes between objective and subjective (i.e., mental) concepts. The objective concept of water is the one that identifies water with H_2O; subjective concepts of water are those we have actually used to think about water—as the colorless, odorless liquid or as the stuff whose triple point is 0° Celsius at 101.3 kilopascals. What we explicate in philosophy is the objective concept of beauty, "the unique unchangeable concept that is and should be denoted by the word's use in treatises on aesthetics" (§1). Notice the "should be."

Second, Bolzano points out that concepts can be coextensive, sometimes by necessity. Parallelograms are quadrilaterals with opposing sides parallel, and parallelograms are quadrilaterals with opposing sides of equal length. Only the former proposition explicates the objective concept of a parallelogram, though it succeeds in part because we can use it to prove the latter. Likewise, water is H_2O, but the stuff that is H_2O is coextensive with the stuff whose triple point is 0° Celsius at 101.3 kilopascals. Subjective, everyday concepts are no help in deciding between these explications of the concept of water. What is helpful is that science explains water's triple point with reference to its molecular structure. The concept of water is the one that identifies it with H_2O because we can use that concept to explain water's triple point.

Third, the adequacy of an explication is to be tested by what Bolzano describes as rigorous introspection. We think hard about a sample of beauty to see whether the thoughts it activates correspond exclusively with the explication that is under review. Sections 2–10 illustrate the procedure in action, and it includes the use of counterexamples, such as the case of Robinson Crusoe in §§4–5 and the case of the historical portrait in §8. However, introspection is not the last bastion of proof. Indeed, Bolzano is open to revisionism; for example, he elsewhere rebuilds the concept of religion from the ground up (2007: 190–92). A key passage of the beauty essay, which closes the discussion of method, is worth quoting in full:

> when developing a concept *in a scholarly context*, we need not doubt whether our explication presents in all its parts the concept that we have always denoted with the same word. What matters is that the concept

is expedient and deserves to serve as a foundation for the disciplines concerned with its object. (§1)

In recognition of this, Bolzano's word, "*Erklärung*," is translated as "explication" rather than "definition." The word also means explanation. The point to keep in mind is that an explication is not merely adequate to introspection; it must serve our practical ends and our enterprise of understanding the world.

Explication requires finesse, as is obvious in §§11–15, which mount the main argument for the explication of beauty. On one hand, Bolzano invites us to intensely introspect while contemplating a beautiful object and to check whether we have a distinct awareness of the elements of the explication. To help us along, he offers three examples: the logarithmic spiral, a fable, and a riddle. On the other hand, he concedes that his explication of beauty is so broad as to fail the introspection test. After a wee bout of hand-wringing about the hurdles to further restricting his explication, he eventually embraces its breadth as a virtue:

> even if our explication expands the meaning of the beautiful, this would certainly not be a bad thing if our concept had some significance of its own, which, it is hoped, will not be denied. Is it not certain that the type of object we have explicated deserves its own *name* either way? (§15)

The explicated phenomenon is the one that serves to relax us after work, enhances our enjoyment of life, and helps our young to develop their minds and thereby contribute to our common advancement. That phenomenon deserves the name of beauty.

(What about reasons to choose Bolzano's preferred explication to coextensive ones? The opening paragraph of §14 cleverly arranges the insights presented in §§2–10 into an alternative explication of the concept of beauty that is coextensive with Bolzano's own. The section then shows that his explication implies the alternative. For this reason, it wins out.)

If Bolzano's concept of beauty is not entirely at home in everyday thinking, then it should figure in treatises in aesthetics. Bolzano's second essay is therefore tasked with classifying the fine arts, so that there is a theory of each art, the topic of a treatise. Each treatise will offer guidance, specific to the art, on how to make beautiful works in the art, thereby vindicating Bolzano's explication of beauty as having an explanatory power that justifies it.

Content: The Fine Arts

By keeping in mind how it completes the case for the explication of beauty, we are less likely to succumb to certain first impressions on reading the essay on the fine arts. The essay is easy to lampoon as an exercise in bookkeeping, as prescriptive and school-teacherly in its harping on guidance and learning, and as obsessively preoccupied with marginal or trivial phenomena. None of this is fair, for the essay brings out how the concept of beauty illuminates broad swaths of human cognition, especially practical (act-oriented) cognition. "The Classification of the Fine Arts" headlines their full diversity, celebrates their entanglement in practical affairs, and sees them as reflecting the conditions of human life. In all this, Bolzano's treatment of the fine arts is no less revisionary than his treatment of beauty: the one boosts the case for the other.

To begin with, let us sketch Bolzano's approach. The fine arts are practices or activities that aim at making works that are fit to be contemplated for their beauty. Is this an instance of Abrams's consumption model, where we understand works of art with reference to a special kind of response? Not quite, as Bolzano denies that the fine arts address Addison's "general Sense and Taste of Mankind." His focus is the activity of the individual artist, who is someone with

> the ability to produce, through his free and intentional acts, objects subsumed under the concept of the beautiful in such a way that their beautiful qualities are the result of his technique, which is, in the production of the object, oriented toward this end [of making objects beautiful] and which is thereby conducted in one way and not in any other (§2).

The first thing to notice here is that the artist is someone with a capacity for performing a type of act. The act type is more basic in Bolzano's scheme than the capacity of the artist. Consequently, we should ask what acts are those of making fine art. The answer is that acts of making fine art are those that aim at beauty; they involve an agent intending to make something beautiful. However—and this is crucial—the beauty must be a product of technique. What that means is not yet spelled out, and Bolzano will soon up the precision, but we can already see that, whatever it is, technique is going to be crucial in explaining why artists act exactly as they do, "in one way and not any other." Could there be any better statement of what Abrams called the "construction model," where we understand works of art in terms of the specificities of makers' practices?

An interesting argument comes along in §8 to show that we should not identify the fine arts with practices for making things whose sole purpose is to be beautiful. That the fine arts are precisely such practices—fit only for making beautiful things—was a well-known solution to the problem of the arts in the eighteenth and nineteenth centuries. Bolzano is having none of it. As he argues, the view "would not permit works of art to differ from one another" (§8). Putting it more modestly, we might say the view entails that there could be no rational explanation of their differences—no explanation of their differences that refers to the specific reasons artists have to make them exactly as they do, in one way and not another. Even better, we might say that the view makes it mysterious why the fine arts and works of art differ in the ways that they so manifestly do. The differences between, say, music and architecture are obvious and interesting. (So interesting that we are simply compelled to confront them anew when we attempt to overcome them through comparisons like "music is liquid architecture.")

In short, beautiful things come into the world in three ways. Some are natural beauties, about which Bolzano says little. Some are human artifacts that are similar to natural beauties inasmuch as they are not products of acts implicating beauty-making intentions. For example, correct moral acts are fully determined by moral reasons: the beauty of a dive into the water to save a drowning child must be coincidental, because it would be appalling to learn that the diver was thinking, mid-dive, of her form as an object of contemplation for bystanders on the pier. Finally, works of fine art are products of acts that implicate beauty-making intentions. Yet those intentions never stand alone; they accompany other artifactual intentions, intentions to make this or that kind of thing. Indeed, for Bolzano, the two sets of intentions can, do, and should support each other, when they are successful.

We get a fresh angle on the same picture when we shift from the perspective of the agent *qua* artist onto the perspective of the agent acting on some other intention. Whatever one is up to, one might add in a beauty-making intention, in the right conditions. True to form, Bolzano gives us a succinct statement. The beauty-making intention is in order only when

> we are dealing with the production of an object that we can allow ourselves time to reflect on and that we seek to preserve and make communicable to others, such that it is reasonable to expect that many people will sooner or later observe it with pleasure and benefit, which will be augmented in proportion to the number of beautiful qualities that we have given it. (§5)

What activities meet these conditions? Or which ones do not? Bolzano proceeds without assuming that the answer is poetry, painting, sculpture, architecture, music, and poetry. On the contrary, what activities count as fine arts is an open question, and open questions are ripe for principled treatment. Given his explication of beauty, no formula is going to narrow down what counts as a fine art. We cannot say, for example, that all and only fine arts produce works with a unified diversity of forms, or that all and only fine arts produce expressions of particularized emotion.

Surprisingly, Bolzano never restates his explication of the beautiful in the course of characterizing an intention to make something beautiful. He leaves it to us to connect the dots. Recall that we are viewing the situation from the perspective of any kind of agent, in conditions where they might supplement their intentions with a further, beauty-making intention. In writing a preface for an edition of Bolzano's essays, I aim to snag my readers' attention, to dispose them to feel sympathetically toward Bolzano, and to assess in broad strokes the significance of his thought for history and for our thinking today. My training in philosophy has equipped me with some reading, reasoning, and writing skills that help me to achieve these aims. So far, though,

I am on a path to writing something that might as well be as dry as dust. Would I not do a better job in accomplishing my aims were I to try to make it beautiful? That does not entail purple prose or a lot of alliteration. Instead, I should make the points that need to be made in a way that occasions pleasure because it triggers a process of conceptual cognition that enables the reader to guess, reliably well, at the points I wish to make, without the rigor of distinct thought, thereby making them aware of the augmentation of their powers of mind. Having added a beauty-making intention to my other intentions, I open the preface by quoting what I hope will be an evocative and revealing tidbit from one of the essays. (If it frustrates instead, then §18 of the beauty essay applies.)

Philosophical writing is on nobody's list of fine arts, even if it can be beautiful (Lopes 2022). For Bolzano, however, it is indeed a fine art. The logic is that beauty is a result of a twist on ordinary cognition, and many types of acts that present objects or events for ordinary cognition are candidates for beauty making. That is, many acts of making things—even prefaces to philosophy books—benefit from the addition of a beauty-making intention. The essay on the fine arts is chock full of examples that confirm how the fine arts' diversity matches that of beauty. The fine arts include parades, fireworks, gymnastics, and horsemanship, but also science and even thinking to oneself, as well as the art of living well. Not to mention the child's visual art of moving to the groove of music.

Time to take stock. On one hand, Bolzano's treatment of the fine arts shares some attractive features with his explication of beauty. He welcomes the sheer diversity of the fine arts, and he insists on their entanglement in practical affairs—the intention to make beautiful builds upon another practical intention. Inasmuch as the intention to make beautiful is an intention to engage creatures who are limited in their faculties but are capable of learning and hence inhabit cultures, the fine arts also reflect the conditions of human life. Carole Maigné puts it nicely: "what surprises him and fills him with enthusiasm is the infinite diversity of human making," about which his stance is "lateral" and "non-hierarchical" (2017: 44). On the other hand, Bolzano's treatment of the fine arts is brazenly revisionary. When we introspect on the arts nowadays, we have thoughts about painting, sculpture, architecture, music, and poetry, plus photography, installation art, landscape architecture, sound art, and fiction. We do not have thoughts of horsemanship or parades, let alone thinking to oneself, philosophy, or biology. It is fair to ask what progress has been made in appealing to a revisionary concept of the fine arts in support of a revisionary concept of beauty.

The argument must be that what vindicates the explication of beauty is that it makes sense of beauty as it figures in treatises on aesthetics, each presenting a theory of a fine art. To make this argument work, each art must be conceived without initial appeal to the explication of the beautiful. Moreover, a few examples drawn from this or that corner of human life will not suffice, because one might reject Bolzano's chosen examples in favor of other examples that echo the narrower concept of the fine arts, which is endemic among us now. For these reasons, Bolzano offers a systematic classification of the arts.

The classification proceeds under four strictures. First, the arts are to be classified without appeal to beauty—beauty comes in only after an art is fully classified. We will say what writing is and then turn to what counts as beautiful writing. Second, the arts are to be viewed as practices of making. For this reason, it makes sense to classify each art as a specific kind of making. That is the third pillar. Conjoining the second and third pillars, we get a fourth. The arts are topics for theories in which practical instruction is part of science (in the broad sense of *Wissenschaft* as including all domains of inquiry). Some activities of making are fine arts because they include practical instruction embodied in a scientific understanding of beauty-making intentions specific to the art. We call such an understanding an "art theory."

Here Bolzano reasonably assumes that human practices of making are cultural practices—they are learned. And what is learned must be a pattern, however complex, that can be taught. Bolzano himself warns against a caricature of learning through "mere rules and written prescriptions" (§4). Learning takes advantage of guidance, which includes historical and biographical writing, studies of examples, and the process of making preparatory drafts of a work (§§1.3, 4.3–4.4). Successful learning makes the guidance you receive part of your "second nature" (§2).

Inasmuch as they include all learned practices of making, the challenge of classifying the arts is mind-boggling. "Our investigation," he writes, "will involve going through all of the products that humans are capable of making through their free and intentional activity" (§7). In order to cut the task down to a manageable size, Bolzano highlights four dimensions of acts of making in each art. First, all acts have purpose. Purpose combines, nests, and chains, of course, so the claim is not that each art has one purpose but rather that we can think of an art partly in terms of the multiple purposes it serves (§8). Second, all acts involve using some means to achieve the purposes in question. Means are tools and also materials, conceived broadly (§9). Third, to understand any act of making, hence any practice of making, we must consider limitations on human action. Bolzano emphasizes the psychological differences between the senses and interpersonal differences in performance, but we might also weigh environmental and even cultural limits on action (§10). Finally, acts and arts can be simple or complex. In simple arts, acts of making can only be performed by solo agents (not collaborating collectives), and they can only be learned through an integral course of study, none of whose parts can be carved off as inessential (§6). For example, painting is not simple because drawing outlines and filling in colors can be assigned to different agents (remember paint by numbers). Music is not simple because it is possible to learn rhythmic patterns without learning melodies. Notice that beauty so far makes no appearance, in compliance with the first pillar.

Having highlighted four dimensions along which we can classify the arts, Bolzano gets down to the classification, which occupies §§11–39 of the essay. He begins with simple arts—arts of pure thought, arts whose products only engage the sense of hearing, and arts whose products only engage the sense of sight—before turning to combinations of these arts. In each case he asks, what are some of the purposes to be achieved? How may they be achieved? Should we note limitations or idiosyncrasies in human performance? Answering these questions explicates the art in question.

That sets the stage to consider whether the art is a fine art. Can and should it be one that is enhanced by an intention to make beautiful? Are its purposes better served, given the available means and the limitations of human performance, when beauty is added to the mix?

If the answer is in the affirmative, then it stands to reason that learning the art should include learning to use the techniques of the art to make beautiful. It is a fine art. The concept of the beautiful must figure in an art theory that completely encapsulates, for practical purposes, our best understanding of it.

Working systematically through the arts in this way, it turns out that almost every art (or activity of making) is a fine art, one whose works can be enhanced by beauty. Therefore, until we acknowledge beauty's role, we will fall short in understanding our lives as practical agents and as agents who learn from each other. We will be apt to over-look how, in general, reasons to make beautiful are already contained in our purposes and the means to achieve them. We will also be apt to overlook particular possibilities for making.

We are wrong to think that systematic thinking inhibits imagi-nation. Paisley Livingston astutely observes that the essay on the fine arts is both "systematic and imaginative" (2016: 334). Some of what amount to predictions have been confirmed. Bolzano correctly bet that we would one day have abstract painting, movies, kinetic sculp-tures, light installations such as *Ganzfeld* by James Turrell, and, more abstrusely, nonmusical sonic works for multiple voices, as in Glenn Gould's contrapuntal radio documentaries (e.g., *The Idea of North*). Even more remarkably, he foresaw that abstract paintings made up of uniform fields of color could not succeed unless they also evoked some intellectual content.

The conclusion to draw is that Bolzano's explication of beauty, pre-cisely because it is so broad, earns its keep. Beauty is at its core what we respond to in a process of learning, augmenting our cognitive powers. The fine arts are activities where we make things, drawing upon what we have learned but also seeking to trigger that same learning process in others. Beauty and the fine arts are together diverse, act-oriented, supremely human phenomena. Together they illuminate how we can and should pursue, and learn to pursue, a level of beauty in anything we do.

Bolzano's two essays in aesthetics modify the consumption model and the construction model so that they are compatible and work in con-cert with one another. To accomplish this, Bolzano upends how his contemporaries framed the problem of the arts. The fine arts do not comprise a sphere separate from the sciences and practical affairs. We must view them very broadly. Does this picture remain hard for us to take on board? The argument here has been that it ultimately bespeaks Bolzano's deepest commitments, to the practicality, diversity, and humanity of beauty and art. Therefore the question to ask is ultimately this: do you share those commitments?

APPENDIX

Bolzano on Kant and Post-Kantian Aesthetics

Having first read the *Critique of Pure Reason* at the age of eighteen, Bolzano engaged throughout his life with Immanuel Kant's contributions across philosophy. In *The New Anti-Kant*, written by František Příhonský under Bolzano's supervision, we read that philosophy had fallen into a period of stagnation until Kant revived in it a spirit of reflection and a zest for new ideas (2014[1850]: 29). Bolzano applauded Kant's foundational distinctions between analytic and synthetic, a priori and a posteriori, and concept and intuition. However, he disputed Kant's accounts of each distinction, as well as most of Kant's doctrines in logic, metaphysics, epistemology, and ethics. Moreover, the disagreement acquired a sharp edge as Bolzano was convinced that Kant had unintentionally wrought a "terrible disaster" on subsequent philosophy and on European society more generally (Příhonský 2014[1850]: 7; Rusnock and Šebestík 2019: 374). So profound was the damage that Bolzano sought to remedy it by critiquing its sources in Kant's writings.

At first glance, Bolzano's aesthetics is an exception to the pattern. His vocabulary is Kantian, and the lexical overlap bespeaks a broad thematic unity. Works of fine art aim at beauty, and beauty involves pleasure in contemplation, which is a particular kind of cognitive operation, one mediating self-awareness. The two philosophers also converge on a vision of beauty and art as distinctively human phenomena, ones that reflect the limits of human cognition. Nonetheless, a closer look is needed. Despite the broad similarity, Bolzano takes issue with every major doctrine of Kant's aesthetics.

Kant

Kant's express aim in *Critique of the Power of Judgment* is to answer the question, How are judgments of taste possible? The question assumes a characterization of judgments of taste. To begin with, a judgment of taste is a feeling of pleasure. Some pleasures are sensory, such as the delicious taste of watermelon. Some are pleasures in a final good (e.g., world peace) or an instrumental good (e.g., a system of microloans). Judgments of taste are neither sensory nor pleasures in the good.

Four features set judgments of taste apart from other pleasures. First, they are disinterested. All pleasures motivate, but disinterested pleasures are ones that do not depend on the existence of the pleasing object or that only motivate contemplation, hence a continuation of the pleasure itself. Second, judgments of taste are universal but nonconceptual. The judgment that this is beautiful is valid for everyone. Yet the reason why it is universally valid has nothing to do with its representing an item as having certain properties that would please anyone. Attributing no specific properties to the item, it is nonconceptual. Third, judgments of taste do not represent an item as having a purpose, but they do represent it as having what Kant calls "the mere form of purposiveness" (2000[1790] 5:221). Fourth, judgments of taste are necessary pleasures: one must or should take pleasure in the beautiful.

Some of these features seem to clash. If judgments of taste are nonconceptual, then they do not represent items as having properties that would make them pleasing. In that case, how can they be universally valid? Kant answers that there is something about us, something in our propensity to respond, that we share in common. Indeed, he argues that judgments of taste are possible just because we have minds that are equipped to have experiences.

How so? We only need part of the story, which concerns the roles played by two mental powers, imagination and understanding. Imagination is a capacity to present sensations; understanding is a capacity to wield concepts. Thus imagination assembles colors, shapes, and fragrances, while understanding applies to the assemblage the concept of a rose. The result is a judgment that this is a rose. Kant maintains that no experience is possible without a process like this.

Sometimes imagination and understanding go into harmonious free play. Imagination presents an assemblage of properties, to which understanding applies a concept, but the process does not halt there. Instead, imagination assembles properties anew, understanding applies a new concept, the process repeating itself, the two powers in balance, neither halting the other. This harmonious free play pleasingly animates the mind, and it displays and draws attention to the mind's working, which is also pleasing. The harmonious free play of imagination and understanding is (or issues in) a judgment that this is beautiful.

Consequently, judgments of taste are possible for the very reasons that explain why experience is possible. They are universally valid because they issue from nothing more than the operation of two powers needed for any experience. Since harmonious free play does not halt with concept application, they are nonconceptual. Being nonconceptual, they do not represent a reproducible condition and so cannot figure in desires to act: they are disinterested. Likewise, being nonconceptual, they cannot represent items as having definite purposes, though they do represent items in a way that is amenable to harmonious free play, which amounts to having a "mere form of purposiveness." Finally, we all must or should take pleasure in how our mental powers operate, and the judgment that this item is beautiful is an exemplary case of that.

A special challenge confronts artists. They must intend to make something, but we cannot find their work beautiful by means of a conceptual judgment that represents it as having a purpose or that might motivate an act. Artists must make items that are apt to put imagination and understanding into harmonious free play. Their work must express what Kant calls an "aesthetic idea," a representation that "stimulates so much thinking that it can never be grasped in a determinate concept," that "gives the imagination cause to spread itself over a multitude of related representations, which let one think more than one can express in a concept determined by words" (2000[1790]: 5:315). Aesthetic ideas animate the harmonious free play of the mind's powers, evoking aesthetic pleasure. It follows that artists must use genius, which is a talent for expressing aesthetic ideas and which cannot be learned, because learning involves concepts.

The arts classify according to media for expressing aesthetic ideas. Aesthetic ideas can be expressed in speech, as in rhetoric and poetry. They can be expressed in images, yielding the plastic and pictorial arts. Expressed in sensation, we get music and the art of color.

Bolzano on Kant

In the second half of the essay on beauty (not included in this edition), Bolzano sizes up the views of more than seventy philosophers, and Kant gets especially close attention. Kant's four features are discussed in order, but Bolzano's critique exploits their interrelations, and, for this reason, it makes sense to start with the central point of disagreement.

Bolzano cannot accept that the response to beauty is nonconceptual. According to Kant, judgments of taste are nonconceptual because the harmonious free play of imagination and understanding outputs nonconceptual judgments. Is it true that all beauty responses issue from a cognitive process with nonconceptual outputs (§38)? One of Kant's own examples is the "intertwined features" of abstract classical patterns (e.g., fig. 3). Bolzano counters that we do not find the patterns beautiful "until we have represented to ourselves, obscurely at least, some rules to which the features correspond—that is, until we have brought them under concepts" (§38). Going further, Bolzano insists that some items, such as mathematical theorems, are purely conceptual and yet beautiful. We can apprehend their beauty only by conceptualizing them.

Figure 3

Kant also takes judgments of taste to represent items as having a "mere form of purposiveness," not as having purpose. Bolzano doubts that this is even possible. Here is how things work:

we conclude that an object before us is produced for a purpose if, after examining all its features, we find that it is suited to achieve something that a reasonable being can want to bring about. We immediately declare this to be the purpose intended by the object's author, and we find its purposiveness to be all the greater the more we perceive how its parts and features contribute their share to bringing about that achievement. As a rule, therefore, the perception of purposiveness always presupposes the perception of a definite purpose. When we cannot discern a purpose, it never occurs to us to suspect purposiveness. (§39)

If that is correct, the question is whether yoking perceived purposiveness with perceived purpose is a problem for understanding beauty. It is not. On one hand, Bolzano holds that one can savor an item's beauty without attributing any purpose to the item. To attribute a purpose to something, one must apply a concept, but Kant also seems to assume the converse, namely that to apply a concept to something one must attribute a purpose to it. This is why judgments of taste in response to the Greek key pattern are supposed to be nonconceptual: the pattern apparently serves no purpose. Bolzano responds that "we seek from beauty—and find in it—not purposes but only rules or concepts" (§39). On the other hand, Bolzano does not take beauty responses to require any apprehension of purposiveness. "Is it true," he asks, "that pleasurable play only occurs when we encounter a form of purposiveness without purpose? Are we not also pleased when, examining an item's regularity, we are fortunate to find, without much time or effort, a rule according to which it is arranged?" (§39). In sum, the concepts of which we are obscurely aware in responding to beauty might be concepts of purposes or of properties seen as suited to serve purposes. Or they might not be.

From the claim that beauty responses are conceptual it follows that not all judgments of taste are universally valid. Not everyone can make the same judgments of taste, for the judgments of taste that someone can make vary with the concepts they have learned. As long as concepts are learned, learning is needed to find an item beautiful, and learning varies, so judgments of taste must vary too. Making matters worse, Bolzano notes that nothing in Kant's argument for universality justifies limiting judgments of taste to cognitive formation: "the argument must be false, because it would prove too much" (§38).

Are judgments of taste necessary pleasures? Propositions are necessary precisely because they are purely conceptual (containing no intuitions). Opposite sides of parallelograms are necessarily equal in length. Every virtue is necessarily beautiful. If judgments of taste are nonconceptual, then how can they be necessary? Kant answers that they have "exemplary" necessity: each is a singular case of a product of a process, the harmonious free play of imagination and understanding, that we all must undergo. Bolzano replies that a response to an item's beauty is contingent upon "a due level of mental training, . . . previous practice in judging objects of the kind, and . . . the opportunity to contemplate the object in question with the requisite attention" (§39*bis*). Unless one is suitably equipped, it is not the case that one must or should judge an item beautiful.

Whereas Kant holds judgments of taste to be nonconceptual yet universal and necessary, Bolzano argues that beauty responses are conceptual, not universal, and contingent upon intellectual formation. What about disinterest?

Here Bolzano meets Kant partway. Pleasure in beauty is not, he agrees, a pleasure in what offers just any advantage. He writes that "insofar as we find an object beautiful, we expect no other advantage apart from the advantage that consists in pleasure arising from the contemplation of its beauty" (§37). At the same time, he rejects Kant's argument that pleasure in contemplation implicates no desires because it is indifferent to the existence of the object contemplated. Surely, he writes, "whenever a beautiful object is real, we desire its continued existence for the very reason that, without it, we could never form a representation of the object with the required vivacity and ease" (§37; also see the essay on beauty §2.3).

At the heart of Bolzano's disagreement with Kant is the nature of contemplation. For Bolzano, pleasure in beauty arises from the same kind of conceptual thinking as occurs in ordinary practical and theoretical contexts. Contemplation begins and ends with concepts; it is not a special play of the powers of mind that never resolves conceptually. Bolzano could not be clearer about this, but Kant casts a long shadow that obscures their differences. For instance, according to one influential commentator on Bolzano, to contemplate is to "set in motion a procedure of exploiting an exemplary object conceptually, making ever finer and finer distinctions, in anticipation of a regularity, in order to keep alternative uses of language available" (Gerhardus 1972: 34). The picture of aesthetic contemplation as conceptually inexhaustible is Kant's, not Bolzano's.

The essay on the classification of the fine arts does not include a discussion of Kant, but it is not hard to draw the contrast. In his thinking about the fine arts, Kant's central commitments are to aesthetic ideas and genius. Artists working in an art form, such as painting, must use the techniques of their art knowledgeably and intentionally. Nevertheless, what they produce is beautiful only if it goes beyond the application of technique and puts in motion the harmonious free play of imagination and understanding. Aesthetic ideas fit the bill, for they overflow conceptual containers. It follows that the competence needed to generate aesthetic ideas cannot reduce to knowledge of technique. Genius is required.

Bolzano's essay on the fine arts is incompatible with both of Kant's commitments. What makes a painting beautiful is its presenting an opportunity to exercise a concept, whether it be a mundane one, such as the concept of a rose, or a richly human one, such as the concept of love. For Bolzano, anything in the presentation that escapes conceptual understanding is frustrating, not pleasing. As a result, what artists do is use the techniques of their art to engage conceptual thought. Unlike scientists and philosophers, they do not compel us to think distinctly about roses or love. That is a point of difference. Yet obscure thought is nonetheless conceptual. For this reason, artists can learn to make beautiful art, following guidance. The overall aim of Bolzano's philosophy of beauty and art is to lay a foundation for theories of the various arts that provide the guidance.

For an interesting measure of the distance separating the two philosophers, consider what each counts among the arts. Since there is no place in science for aesthetic ideas and the genius that generates them, a beautiful science would be "absurd" (2000[1790]: 5:305), and the same goes for what we would now consider the arts of design. Kant punctiliously endorses the eighteenth-century list of the fine arts. Bolzano blows it up. Mathematics, the sciences, and philosophy can be practiced as fine arts, as can any human enterprise where value is added by inviting contemplation that produces pleasure because some learning is happening. As Bolzano is well aware, learning is not confined to the academy; it occurs in all kinds of practical enterprises too.

Bolzano on Aesthetics after Kant

On the very first page of their biography of Bolzano, Paul Rusnock and Jan Šebestík commend his "deep respect for the work of his predecessors, even when he thinks them profoundly mistaken" (2019: 1). Bolzano's focus on the specifics of Kant's aesthetics is a sign of respect, as is his leaving it to us to trace the deeper source of their disagreement in their pictures of human cognition. When it comes to the "terrible disaster" that Kant might have wrought on subsequent aesthetics, Bolzano is equally circumspect. He concludes his critique of Kant's teachings with the remark that they "greatly affected subsequent treatments of the theory of the beautiful," adding that "time will tell whether the effect was beneficial" (§40). Time has since passed. Perhaps, with the benefit of hindsight, we can see better what it was in the nineteenth-century reaction to Kant that worried Bolzano and that he hoped to correct. Here is one proposal.

According to Jean-Marie Schaeffer (2000: ch. 1), a single line of thought—a line of thought about art—drives German aesthetics in the wake of Kant: (1) If art is concerned with beauty, then there can be no theory of art. And (2) if there can be no theory of art, then there can be no speculative theory of art. However, (3) we need a speculative theory of art. Therefore, (4) art is not concerned with beauty. Assumption (1), namely that art is concerned with beauty, is an implication of Kant's aesthetics. Judgments of taste overflow conceptual containment, so the best we can do by way of theory is explain how they are possible—we cannot circumscribe what it is in works of art that determines their beauty. Assumption (2) is trivial. The motivation behind (3) was, as Schaeffer explains, a reaction to enlightenment philosophy, which was seen as having desacralized religion and as having invited an invasion of science into European intellectual culture. Salvation was to be found in art and philosophy, both conceived as modes of access to special truths. However, philosophers disagreed loudly about the details, for each offered a substantive theory of the special, speculative function of art. All the same, they could agree that, given (1), no such theory could make appeal to beauty or to judgments of taste. Art and beauty had to part company.

On all of this, Bolzano is out of step with his contemporaries. He secularizes religion, reducing it to ethics, and he sees ethics, science, philosophy, and the arts as best striving together for social progress. He must therefore pull the plug on the line of thinking laid out above, before it gets to assumption number (3).

That means taking on assumption number (1), which is Kant's legacy. To deny this premise is to assert precisely that the arts are concerned with beauty and that there can be theories of the arts. Since responses to beauty in art are contained conceptually, we can, after all, craft guidance for making beautiful art. We can have theories of the arts. Theories of the arts will not assign to them a common speculative function; they will organize the arts around specific techniques of making beautiful things that serve any number of practical and theoretical purposes.

As a result, we need not limit the arts to a small number of very special practices, and we may welcome their permeability into all arenas of human thought and endeavor. By challenging a line of thought anchored in Kant, Bolzano charts an alternative to mainstream nineteenth-century aesthetics.

On the Concept of the Beautiful

Preface

The fact that I have decided to fill so many pages with the analysis of a single concept might, for some, seem to demand explanation. I can only reply that this concept seems to me to be of particular importance and, further, that the analysis of concepts is a matter that always demands expansive inquiries if one is to go beyond merely *saying* that the concept is reducible to its parts and actually convince the reader, thus also taking care to demonstrate that the attempts at explicating the concept that have been made so far are lacking in one way or another. After I have completed this essay on the fundamental concept of *aesthetics*, I will not deem it necessary to proceed with such thoroughness in the essays that follow.

1

In this essay I will seek to *explicate* or *define* a concept known and used by us all, namely, the concept that we associate with the word "beautiful," so long as we understand this word in its proper sense, the sense used in various *treatises on aesthetics*. By "explicating" or "defining," I understand nothing other than establishing whether the concept of the beautiful is simple or complex and, if it happens to be complex, determining the other concepts it is composed of and their specific relations to one another. Thus, I hardly aim to forge some new concept wholly unknown to my readers. Rather, I simply aim to elucidate the constituents of a concept that they, in their own minds, have already formed, even though they might not have a clear idea of how they formed it, or they might have simply forgotten. We can find numerous examples of the fact that we are sometimes unable to clearly explicate each and every part of a concept that we ourselves have developed. How else are we to explain the fact that we are so often stumped when someone asks us to explain what we mean when we use a certain concept, even one we make use of every day? And how to explain the fact that we are so seldom able to agree on the definition of such concepts? Is it even necessary for me to say that the concept of the *beautiful* belongs to those concepts the meaning of which is contested and the clarification of which has been attempted so many times? Or that it is generally seen as one of the most difficult concepts? Of course, in the following essay, I will view it as my duty to refer to the most important among these attempts and to show why I have not been able to remain satisfied with any of them.[1]

But before beginning my analysis of the concept of the beautiful, it seems necessary for me to make my readers aware of some presuppositions that will inform my entire investigation, because, if they are unable to agree with me on these points, then it is hardly to be expected that they will agree with me on anything that follows.

1. When meditating on some object or when thinking in general, we often *alter* our thoughts, going from one thought to the next or from one judgment to its *opposite*. Such alterations might be called *shifts in our thoughts*, shifts that in a certain sense are not harmful and are even unavoidable if we want to increase or improve our knowledge. However, it is impossible to speak of such *shifts* or *alterations* when discussing what I call *propositions and truths in themselves*, or *objective*

---

1. [Bolzano undertakes this review in §§26–57, not translated here.]

truths and propositions, or, similarly, when discussing what I call *concepts and representations in themselves,* or *objective concepts and representations.*[2] It is a very simple matter to draw a distinction between propositions and representations *in themselves* (or *objective* propositions and representations) and *subjective* or *thought* propositions and representations (judgments and so forth), which are simply the forms in which the former *appear* in the minds of thinking beings. The simplicity of making this distinction is evidenced by the fact that everyone has some understanding of it. For example, everyone understands me when I say, "In philosophy, there is only one *concept in itself* designated by the word *God,* even though there are an infinite number of different *concepts* and *representations,* some clearer than others, some incorrect, that individual *human beings* associate with this word." In the first part of the sentence, I spoke of the concept of God in its objective meaning; in the latter, in its subjective meaning. Even though this distinction makes itself known to us in various ways, it has yet to be elucidated. Most importantly, the distinguishing features of objective propositions and representations remain to be subjected to rigorous philosophical analysis. That there is such a lack has been made particularly clear by the fact that the attempts I have made to address myself to these problems in the first two volumes of my *Theory of Science* remain the only attempts to do so.[3] If this distinction is grasped and admitted, one will, it is hoped, grant that, although *thought* propositions and representations can be altered and change into their opposite (because they are thought by particular thinking beings at particular points in time), *propositions in themselves* and their constituents—the *concepts and representations in themselves*—are not subject to change, because they are not part of *being, existence,* or *actuality,* and so cannot undergo change. Thus, so long as we seek to discuss *concepts* and *representations* in their *objective sense,* we may never speak of a transition of one concept to another,

---

2. [See Bolzano 2014(1837): §19 and §§48–49. Concepts are a species of representations and representations are components of propositions.]

3. And nonetheless, I believe this attempt clearly shows that the πρῶτον ψεῦδος [basic error] of recent philosophy has been occasioned by the lack of a clear notion of the *concept in itself,* the latter having been at once confused with *thoughts,* then with the *things* that are its object.

of a concept turning into its opposite, or of a *dialectical progression* of such concepts and representations. As our current aim is to explicate the concept of the *beautiful*, we must shift our focus away from the subjective, alterable concept that we have associated with this word in the various phases of our lives, as children, adolescents, and so forth, and turn our attention toward the unique unchangeable concept that is and should be denoted by the word's use in treatises on aesthetics. As such, we are dealing with nothing other than the determination of a *concept in the objective sense*, although, if we are to be able to make judgments about this concept at all, it must certainly appear to us in our minds—that is, as a subjective concept. The concept to be explicated in this essay—that is, the concept that is to be broken up into its constituents (if it is, indeed, a complex concept)—is a *concept in itself.* As such, we have no reason to speak of the concept's movement, of its gradual transition into another concept, of its sudden shift into its opposite, or of anything of the sort.

2. If we want to safeguard our thinking from error and keep ourselves from being responsible for others misunderstanding us, confusing them more than teaching them anything, then we must avoid using one and the same word to denote one thing one minute and another thing the next; that is, we must avoid using the same word to denote first one concept, then another. Thus, we may only develop a single *explication* or *definition* of each one of our *words* or, more precisely, of the *concepts denoted* by them. It is a miserable state of affairs when philosophers (particularly those of recent times, such as J. H. Fichte[4] when defining the concept of the *absolute*) give us *multiple explications* of one and the same word or concept, believing that a second is *richer in content* than the one that preceded it or that the one follows from one *perspective*, the other from another *perspective*. Contrary to what they claim, it is not one and the same concept. Rather, it is clear that these philosophers want to denote multiple concepts with a single word in a way that must result in nothing but confusion. For the explications they give do not diverge from one another simply in the purely

---

4. [The original text has "J. H. Fichte" here; the Athenäum edition has "I. H. Fichte." However, "J. G. Fichte" is also plausible, since Bolzano criticizes him in §45 (not included in this translation).]

contingent expressions they are couched in or in their varying degrees of rigor, as if the one merely contained the most readily apparent parts of the concept, the other elaborating on its finer points. Even if the divergent explications concerned concepts that I call equivalent or interchangeable concepts[5]—that is, concepts that encompass the same objects—they would still be *different* concepts. So it is an error to confuse them with one another, viewing them as one rather than considering their intrinsic, often essential differences. To draw a comparison with a science that for millennia has been seen as an unattained, even unattainable, ideal for all the others, it has never been permitted in mathematics to treat mutually inclusive concepts as definitions of one and the same concept. That would be like saying that the concept of a quadrilateral with *sides of equal length* and the concept of a quadrilateral with *parallel sides* are both definitions of one and the same concept—namely, that of the parallelogram. Rather, mathematics takes up one of these concepts as a definition and then demonstrates that the other concept has the same extension. Let us work with the same precision when attempting to explicate the concept of the beautiful. And when we have reached the point where we believe we have found an explication that corresponds with our understanding of this concept, let us not follow the same path as those who amend their explications with a second and a third, claiming that it is also possible to come up with the same concept by combining certain other attributes that differ from those that the explication originally contained.

3. That concepts (or representations in general) can be divided into the *simple* and the *complex*, the latter being a specific way of relating the former to one another, is not a sign of barbarity (as *Hegel* liked to say).[6] Rather, it is a theory wholly in line with truth, a theory confirmed by our innermost consciousness and by the most pregnant examples. Does not our own mind tell us that some concepts can only be got at by combining various other concepts with one another? For instance, you see a clay jar the color or fragility of which reminds you of various items you recently saw that were made out of India rubber. You are certain, however, that these two representations, taken together, result

5. [Bolzano 2014(1837): §96(b).]

6. [Hegel 2010: 542–43. See also Bolzano 2014(1837): §65.]

in the representation of a jar made of India rubber instead of clay. Thus, combining the concepts of India rubber and jar you get the concept of an *elastic jar*. Of course, we do not always have a clear consciousness of the constituents of complex concepts. This is particularly the case with concepts we developed in early childhood, concepts that we gradually acquired rather than having learned in a single stroke, or words the meaning of which we only deciphered after hearing them used many times. But we cannot seriously doubt the fact that all these concepts must either be simple or composed of other concepts (to which some sensory impressions might be added). This is true because, if we are unable to view a representation as simple, then what else could it consist of but other representations? We certainly cannot permit ourselves to be coaxed into the conviction still held by many logicians that every *attribute* of the *object* of a concept must also be a *constituent of the concept itself.* Although most of the constituents of a concept represent attributes that are generally found in the objects of the concept, it is certain that the constituents of the concept need not include concepts that represent all the qualities of the objects. That cannot be true simply because, if it were, then the content of every concept would be endless, because the set of qualities of every single object, and even every species of objects, is endless. For instance, the concept of a "human body" is simply the concept of the body of human beings—that is, of sensible, rational creatures who inhabit the earth. We certainly have a concept of this body's qualities when we consider the fact that it has such and such limbs and organs, and these qualities are certainly part of the object understood by the concept of a human body. But these qualities are in no way referred to in the content of this concept. Thus, if we take it upon ourselves to explicate a concept, then we must first determine whether this concept is simple or complex. If it is complex, we must then enumerate the *sum of its constituents*, but in no way the *sum of the qualities* shared by its objects. We only need to list those qualities actually contained in the concept itself. Our explication of the concept of *the beautiful* will proceed in the same way. We must determine whether the concept is simple or complex, but it is in no way our duty to elucidate the *entirety* of the qualities of the beautiful. It is wholly sufficient if those qualities not stated in our explication can be deduced from it.

4. From what has been said thus far, it should be readily apparent that explicating a *concept in itself*, such as the concept of the beautiful, is no easy task, nor is convincing others of the correctness of such an explication. If we claim that the concept in question is *simple*, then we can only defend this claim by demonstrating that any attempt to produce this concept by means of combining other concepts with one another fails. And we can only do this in two ways, either by showing that such attempts are ultimately circular, that they contain the concept in the explication of the concept itself, or by showing that they end up explicating a concept wholly different from the concept in question. By contrast, if we claim that the concept in question is complex, explicating its constituents and the ways they stand in relation to one another, then we are obliged to demonstrate that the extension of the concept resulting from the combination of these parts is neither *lesser* nor *greater* than the concept we set out to elucidate. We can only prove this by showing that the concept we have analyzed can be applied to each and every object contained by the concept in question, no more and no less. This we can only do by showing (1) that every quality attributed to the objects of the concept in question can also be deduced from our concept and, conversely, (2) that every quality that can be deduced from our concept can be found in the objects of the concept in question. And even if we accomplish all of this, we still have not demonstrated that our explicated concept really is the same as the concept in question, because they could be *equivalent concepts*. The only means we have to free ourselves of this last bit of doubt and *convince ourselves* is to inquire as to whether our understanding finds the concept adequate. And the only way we can convince *our reader* is to ask him to do the same. The only way to make such an inquiry is to undertake such rigorous introspection that we become aware of the thought processes activated in us by the concept in question. This makes it possible for us to ask whether these thoughts correspond with or diverge from our explication. We can assume with greater probability that we have come across the right explication the more we engage in such introspection and the more convinced we become that our explication corresponds exclusively with the thoughts activated by the concept in question. But such introspection is not for everyone, and it is a capacity that can only be acquired if we have practiced it from our youth

onward, and even then only if we have never permitted ourselves to *deliberately* conceal our innermost thoughts from ourselves. Someone who has never undertaken such intense introspection or who has never had the good intention of doing so will always contradict what we say. And in a certain sense, they will be right in claiming that their mind has no notion of what we have developed in our explication. This is the sort of predicament we are faced with when the last bastion of proof lies in our consciousness alone. But we can at least find some solace in the fact that, when developing a concept *in a scholarly context*, we need not doubt whether our explication presents in all its parts the concept that we have always denoted with the same word. What matters is that the concept is expedient and deserves to serve as a foundation for the disciplines concerned with its object. This matter depends on considerations of a completely different kind, which we can fortunately decide for very plausible reasons that are not subject to contradiction.

2

Now that these preliminaries are over with, I would like to begin my determination of the concept of the beautiful with some *negative propositions*, simply in order to get some things that *are not contained* in this concept out of the way. The concept of the beautiful is not the same as the concept of the *good*, nor as that of the *gratifying*, nor as that of the *charming*. None of these concepts has the same *extension* as that of the beautiful. This is to say that none of them are *equivalent concepts* of the beautiful, not to speak of the impossibility of them having the same constituents (the same *content*).

1. Concerning the good: I wish neither to affirm nor to contest the fact that all *truly good* or *ethical* things possess some sort of beauty. I would also like to make clear that I am of the conviction that nothing *evil* can be called beautiful simply by virtue of the fact that it is evil. Nevertheless, the difference between the sphere of the beautiful and that of the good is so great that we must not lose sight of it. And from this it follows, of course, that the constituents of these concepts must also differ from one another. It is undeniable that we find many

objects beautiful without associating them with the laws of morality in any way whatsoever. Who would claim that our wonder, when contemplating the beauty of some sight, of a building, a flower, or the harmony of music, compels us to find some sign of the laws of morality in these same objects—or that we only find these objects *beautiful* because of their moral content? It might be true that the most perfect beauty may only be attributed to beings who, like human beings and other higher spirits, are not only capable of attaining moral perfection but also actually attain it. And we should be praised when we are able to keep ourselves from being bedazzled by the beauty of people who nevertheless lack moral sensibility. But we should not believe that our virtues are diminished if we admit that nonmoral beings can also be recognized as having some degree of beauty and that the sphere of the beautiful thus extends to all sorts of objects that do not fall into the sphere of the good.

2. The difference between the concepts of the *beautiful* and the *gratifying* is no less apparent. If we do not take the gratifying in the same way as Kant, who goes against the word's everyday use by limiting it to "what pleases the senses"[7] (which we could call *sensory gratification*), then the concept extends to every object that pleases us for any reason whatsoever—that is, every object that causes us pleasure. We no doubt presume that everything *beautiful* is capable of bringing us pleasure under certain circumstances, namely, when we direct our attention toward it. And we certainly do not feel compelled to call things beautiful that are wholly incapable of bringing us any sort of pleasure. The beautiful is thus indisputably an object that *could gratify*, even if it does not in fact gratify. But the reverse—namely, that everything that can gratify deserves to be called beautiful—does not hold. Those familiar with the authentic sense of the word in no way consider beautiful those things that are merely gratifying to our *senses*, things that do not demand any higher capacities than those we attribute to *animals*, fascinating us by the impressions they make on our senses. They thus deem it false when somebody claims, for instance, that the taste of an apple is beautiful merely because it gratifies the senses. Thus, the concept of the

---

7. [Kant's phrase is "what pleases the senses in sensation" (2000[1790]: 5:205)].

gratifying, or even the concept of *what can gratify*, has the same relation to the concept of the beautiful as a higher concept does to a lower one.

3. Despite what Kant says,[8] I have no reservations about claiming that all, or at least most, beautiful objects are *charming* to a certain degree and that they thus evoke a certain *desire* in us. What is more natural than to desire the repetition of a pleasure afforded to us by an object we have deemed beautiful? If the presence of the beautiful object is necessary for us to obtain an adequate representation of it, this desire will bring about the further desire to have that object in our reach. Thus, if we call everything that leaves us with a certain desire *charming*, then we will have a hard time disputing the fact that beautiful objects are also charming objects; "the charm of beauty" is indeed a most common expression. But the reverse does not hold: that not every charming object is beautiful need not be expounded upon. The number of objects that charm our senses and that nobody who understands the concept of beauty would call beautiful is no doubt endless!

3

But if it is true that everything beautiful can be a source of gratification for us and that it can be *pleasing* under certain circumstances, then we must ask in what way or for what reasons can a beautiful object bring us pleasure, if it indeed deserves to be called a *beautiful* object, and what conditions must be met so that we may rightfully call it beautiful. I believe it is correct to say that this pleasure can be brought about in no other way than by the mere *contemplation* of the object. If we want to make a judgment regarding the *pure* beauty of an object, then we must leave aside many things: all the sensations the object can cause in us when we allow it to affect us to a degree beyond that necessary to obtain a mere *representation* of it, all the sensations that arise in us when we permit the object to affect us in a way beyond that necessary for the object's mere contemplation, and, finally, the possibility of *altering* the object in some arbitrary way, *relating* it to ourselves, and so

---

8. [Kant 2000(1790): 5:223–26.]

forth. We must dedicate ourselves to the question of whether the mere *representation* of the object that arises out of our contemplation of it is sufficient to please us. If it is not capable of doing so, then we may call the object many things, but not *beautiful*.

4

Should not this attribute of the beautiful be considered a constituent of the concept of the beautiful? Further, does it not make up the entirety of the concept itself? In that case, every object capable of pleasing us by its mere contemplation would have to be called beautiful. Is this true? I do not think so. I think there are countless things the mere contemplation of which pleases us without us being able to attribute even the slightest bit of beauty to them: all things gratifying to our senses; all things that promise us some *benefit*. We view these things with more or less pleasure, but do we call these things beautiful for that reason? It was certainly with the greatest joy that Campe's Robinson viewed the jagged stone with an oblong hole bored into it that he found on his island.[9] He might have called this find *precious, grand,* even *incomparable,* but he would certainly not have called this object *beautiful,* at least not in the sense of the word used in aesthetics. Thus it is clear that the concept that results from this single attribute of the beautiful is much too broad and that we must therefore limit our concept in some way by adding more attributes. We can find more attributes in two ways: either by closely examining the *characteristics* of the contemplation occasioned by beautiful objects or by trying to give a more precise account of the type of *pleasure* that we experience when contemplating a beautiful object, in that we attempt, for instance, to identify the specific *reason* why we experience this pleasure. Possibly, however, our investigation will have to take up both lines of inquiry.

---

9. [Bolzano refers here to Joachim Heinrich Campe's *Robinson der Jüngere* (1779–1780), an adaptation for children of Defoe's novel.]

5

Let us first direct our attention toward the *particular characteristics* of the contemplation of beautiful objects; that is, let us ask what the *content* of this contemplation is. What aspects of an object do our thoughts engage with such that we experience the beauty of that object? The mere fact that the answer to this question is not universally known and that we can thus raise it as a legitimate question reveals a *peculiarity* of the sort of contemplation in question. It demonstrates that the thoughts involved in our contemplation of the beautiful must be formed with such swiftness and ease *that we, in most cases, are not distinctly conscious of them*. Consider what it would be like if we were capable of once again bringing to awareness the representations, judgments, and inferences involved in contemplating a beautiful object, *saying to ourselves that we have these thoughts*. Would not everybody then be able to say precisely what aspects of an object our thoughts engage with when we find that object beautiful? Or would we at least be able to recall just those thoughts *common to all* our contemplations of beautiful objects? So this too must be an attribute of the beautiful: we derive pleasure from the contemplation of beautiful objects, *a contemplation formed with such ease and swiftness that we need not be distinctly conscious of the thoughts involved in it*. In expressing myself in this way I also wish to state that I do not believe that a beautiful object stops pleasing us if we consciously articulate all the thoughts involved in its contemplation. This is certainly not true, even if many have expressed themselves this way and a few have really thought it to be true. I simply wish to make the claim that an essential aspect of the beautiful is that the thoughts evoked by the beautiful object develop with such ease that we are capable of thinking these thoughts to their end without having *to be conscious* of every single one for itself. In other words, we must be able to think these thoughts to their end without having to make a judgment about each one for itself or even having to make each thought the object of awareness. I think that this is a necessary aspect of that specific sort of pleasure derived from contemplating beautiful objects, which we call *pleasure in the beautiful*. If, on the contrary, the thoughts occasioned by an object are very cumbersome and difficult, if we have to be clearly conscious of all the judgments and inferences involved, then we hardly think of pleasure—or at least not of pleasure in the beautiful. If one is willing to grant me this point, then one admits that the attribute of beauty discussed here is a *universally valid* attribute. However, determining whether this attribute is a *constituent* of the concept of the beautiful is contingent upon the consideration of two factors: we must ask ourselves whether the concept that results from this attribute's combination with the constituents we have already named is not *redundant*. Or, if the concept's extension is too broad, we must ask ourselves whether the attributes that remain to be determined are merely going to end up being burdensome additions that contribute nothing substantial to the concept itself. The concept that results from this combination can be explicated as follows: we may call an object *beautiful* that can bring us pleasure by its mere contemplation, a contemplation that we carry out with *such ease that we need not be distinctly conscious of all the individual thoughts involved in it.* One can hardly claim that this concept contains superfluous parts (beyond the *words* themselves, where it is in a certain sense impossible to avoid superfluity if one does not wish to break all the rules of grammar and usage). It is also clear, however, that the concept's extension is too broad, because it is certainly not true that every object that pleases us by its mere contemplation should be called beautiful (even if we carry out this contemplation swiftly and with ease). Our friend Robinson did not need to arduously mull over all the important things that the stone could do for him. He will have certainly derived pleasure from viewing the stone without, as we said, calling it beautiful.

6

Thus, we must seek out more attributes of the beautiful. Looking back at the way we discovered the attribute of the beautiful explicated in the previous section, it is clear that we did not attempt to answer the question that we tasked ourselves with at the beginning of that section but simply asked how posing such a question was possible in the first place. We asked: what is the *content* of the contemplation that the enjoyment of the beautiful occasions us to engage in? The very fact that we were able to pose this question led us to the following conclusion: it must be the case that we do not have a distinct consciousness of the thought processes involved in such contemplation. This feature of the beautiful only touches upon the *form* of our contemplation, saying nothing about its *content*. Nevertheless, we should welcome this insight, because it reveals an important attribute of the beautiful. As it is clear that we have not explicated all the attributes of the concept in question, it seems reasonable that we make a serious attempt to see if we are not able to answer the question we posed to ourselves, because every correct answer we are able to give will reveal another attribute of the beautiful. So, if, in contemplating a beautiful object, we merely contemplate its beauty and nothing else, then what exactly are our thoughts occupied with in this contemplation? The first answer I would like to give to this question is merely a negative determination: when enjoying the beautiful, *our thoughts are not simply occupied with a relation that the object has to us as individuals*. It is clear that whenever we call an object *beautiful*, we do not do so simply on the basis of a *relation that it has to us alone as individuals*. Rather, we always believe ourselves justified in maintaining the expectation that others who stand in a wholly different relation to the object can and should find the object beautiful too. As *Kant* has shown, all aestheticians presume (and their entire academic discipline rests on this presumption) that *our judgments about beauty make a certain claim to universal validity*[10]—but, I emphasize, only a *certain* claim to universal validity. It is clear that determining the nature of this *universal validity* will greatly aid us in finding the true concept of the beautiful. But no scholar of aesthetics [*Ästhetiker*] has ever made the claim that every object we *human beings* find beautiful must also be *felt* to be beautiful by all other sensory beings without exception. It has always been almost universally agreed that beings on a lower level than human beings, namely, animals, have no capacity for the feeling of the beautiful. Most also agree that there are many significant differences in the subtlety and correctness of tastes from one person to the next. Moreover, most also agree that the capacity to make judgments about the beautiful, and hence the capacity to derive

___

10. [Kant 2000(1790): 5:211–12.]

enjoyment from the contemplation of the same, can only be gradually acquired and thus naturally demands that we *develop* our cognitive powers and that we *exercise* our capacity to judge. Finally, as regards *higher spiritual beings*, one has never risked claiming that they have no *knowledge* of the beautiful and are therefore incapable of making judgments about it and distinguishing it from its opposite. But most have doubted whether the contemplation of the beautiful would bring them any *joy*. Some have gone even further, not simply doubting this fact but decisively denying it.[11] Only in the following sections will we be able to determine whether we should integrate some, or even all, of the hitherto outlined attributes into our concept of the beautiful, thus granting them the status of *constituents*. But one thing is clear: the remarks made so far have certainly provided us with useful insights into the essence of the beautiful. In this regard, we may sum up the two types of considerations we have ventured to make: the first has to do with the *content* of the contemplation occasioned by a beautiful object, whereas the second has to do with the *source* of the pleasure we experience when contemplating the beautiful. Concerning the content of this contemplation, we assume that human beings must first develop their cognitive powers in order to be able to enjoy the contemplation of the beautiful and to make judgments about it. Concerning the source of this gratification, we assume that cognitive powers *much higher* than those of humankind might not weaken the capacity to make *judgments* about the beautiful but most certainly diminish or even nullify the capacity to derive *pleasure* from it. If we admit both of these assumptions and attempt to discover their cause, then we will certainly be able to make important inferences concerning the *content*

---

11. Who would not think of the words of that man who was one of the most discerning judges of the beautiful but was also one of the great masters of producing it?

Your *knowledge* you do share with spirit minds far vaster,

'Tis *Art*, O Man, you have alone!

[Bolzano's emphasis, Friedrich Schiller, "The Artists" (1789), translated by Marianna Wertz, Schiller Institute, https://archive.schillerinstitute.com/transl/trans_schil_1poems.html#the_artist.] By *Art* one must understand only that art has to do with *feeling*. Only the pleasure that accompanies the contemplation of the beautiful is an exclusive characteristic of our species.

of our contemplation of beautiful objects and the *source* of the pleasure
derived from it. Let us attempt both.

7

We again raise the question: what exactly are our thoughts occupied
with when we contemplate the beautiful? But let us now consider the
question in light of the fact that we first obtain the capacity to judge
and enjoy the beautiful only after we have exercised and to some degree
developed our mental powers for this purpose. First of all, let us ask:
what do we do when contemplating an object that we do not view
as a means of satisfying our immediate needs? What do we do when
engaging in contemplation that we intend to be nothing other than
mere contemplation? In such situations we undoubtedly set ourselves the
task of determining *what exactly the thing we have before us is*. But ask-
ing what a thing is means nothing more than looking for a *concept* (or,
what is ultimately the same, for a *representation* or *rule*) from which
the features of the thing can be deduced. Thus, should not the task we
set for ourselves when contemplating a *beautiful* object be exactly the
same? Should we not attempt (whether or not we are fully aware of it)
to come up with a concept that contains the entirety of the object's features, either directly or in such a way that they can be readily inferred
from it? When contemplating a beautiful object, we may certainly form
such a concept or representation. But we must be more precise and
ask whether the representation is *simple* or *complex*. If it is simple, we
must ask whether this representation is one that *exclusively* represents
the object being considered and nothing else—that is, whether a mere
intuition of the object is sufficient.[12] And if it is complex, we must ask
whether this complex representation is a *composite* or a *pure* concept.
This matter clarifies itself when we take into account the fact we are
dealing with here.[13] This shows us clearly that mere *intuitions* are insuf-

---

12. [An intuition is a simple representation with a singular extension, representing
exactly one item.]

13. [That is, the fact that our cognitive powers have been exercised and developed.]

ficient for conceptualizing beautiful objects, because children and even animals can have mere intuitions. If our contemplation of the beautiful and our ability to distinguish it from its opposite were based on nothing but mere intuitions, we would be forced to admit that children and even animals have an eye for the beautiful. There is only one conclusion to be drawn from the assumption that the contemplation of the beautiful presupposes that our powers of cognition be developed to some extent, namely, that such contemplation sets all of our cognitive powers in motion: in addition to our *power of intuition*, also *memory*, our *power of imagination*, our *understanding*, our *power of judgment*, and even our *power of reason*.[14] In order to recognize a beautiful object as such, we must begin with the *intuitions* related to it (if indeed it is an object that can be perceived with the senses). But we must also subsume these intuitions under *concepts of the understanding*, showing that their object has such and such *qualities*. We must therefore not allow ourselves to be satisfied with an explication of the *perceived qualities*. We must also use our *power of imagination* to represent certain other qualities such that, by combining the latter with the former, we obtain a *concept* (pure or composite) from which the rest of the object's qualities can be deduced, including those revealed to us by focused observation. But, when forming a concept, we must not allow ourselves to be guided by mere chance. Rather, we must use our *powers of judgment and reason* in order to carefully select the most adequate features from those that our imagination presents us with. And all of that must be carried out so swiftly and with such ease that we need not be distinctly conscious of the entire process, saying to ourselves that we are doing it. We learned in §5 how correct this is. But, in truth, only after having explained all of this does it become clear why we only *gradually* obtain the capacity to recognize the beautiful and sense it with delight, why the development of this capacity requires both the *exercise* and

---

14. Listing so many powers of mind is, I hope, justified by what I have said elsewhere on the topic, particularly in my *Theory of Science* [Bolzano 2014(1837)]. The prejudice that one has explained a particular thing by merely conceptualizing the power that brings it forth has been particularly ruinous for some academic disciplines, especially psychology. Nevertheless, it is equally true that those who want to hear nothing of powers in the plural, whether those of simple beings or the mind, go too far.

development of our powers, especially our cognitive powers. Because only an imagination capable of presenting a *plethora of possible features* of an object will be able to form an adequate image of the object in question. Only well-developed *powers of judgment and reason* will be able to know which of the imagined qualities the object really has. Only a mind that has practice engaging in such contemplation will be able to conceptualize the object with such swiftness and ease that it need not be distinctly conscious of all the individual representations, judgments, and inferences involved.

8

We set out to determine the content of the contemplation that accompanies our enjoyment of the beautiful, whether we are distinctly conscious of this content or not. We discovered another universally valid attribute of the beautiful. Let us now find out whether combining it with the results of our inquiry up to this point allows us to sufficiently explicate the concept of the beautiful. This will allow us to continue on to our second task (§6),[15] presuming that there is a demonstrated need to do so. I will demonstrate that there is indeed such a need by showing that even if we combine all the attributes developed thus far, the concept that results is still too broad. If there is one single object that has the sum of these attributes but that is not itself beautiful, then the need to continue our inquiry will have been demonstrated. I hope that my readers will accept the claim that every faithful depiction of a historically important person in an image is an example of such an object, even though the person portrayed was in no way beautiful. If they were not beautiful, then we will not be able to find the image beautiful (so long as it is faithful to them). And yet such an image might have all of the attributes we have described thus far. Nobody will dispute the fact that contemplating such an image affords a particular pleasure: on the one hand, a faithful representation of the facial features of such a remarkable person expands and confirms our physiognomic

---

15. [That is, the task of identifying the source of pleasure in the beautiful.]

knowledge; on the other hand, it allows us to make certain inferences about the person's character. Equally indisputable is the fact that we need not have a distinct consciousness of all the thoughts that flit before our minds when we contemplate such an image; after all, we are not always capable of readily identifying the features by means of which we recognize various characters. And just as certain is the fact that the pleasure derived from contemplating such an image does not have its roots in the particular relation that the image has to us as individuals: the image does not please us by granting us a personal benefit but by satisfying an interest that thousands could and should have. Thus, as with a beautiful object, we may also demand that every person with more or less developed cognitive powers will experience the existence and, indeed, the contemplation of such an image with pleasure. Finally, my readers will certainly admit that a portrait is no simple object, containing as it does a whole series of qualities that do not mutually determine one another; they will thus also admit that forming a concept of such an object is no easy task. The point is made clearer if we demand that the contemplating person grasp the *singularity* and *significance* of every facial feature, which for its part necessitates the concentration of all our cognitive powers and a great deal of experience and training. This alone demonstrates that our investigation has not yet provided us with enough attributes to form a concept that would have even the same extension as the concept of the beautiful. We must therefore continue our search. To this end, the best we can do is to carry out the task we set for ourselves.

9

As our goal now is to investigate the *sources of the pleasure in the beautiful*, it seems appropriate first to raise the question: *what in general can serve as a source of delight and pleasure for us and for all other finite beings?* We may only speak of *finite* beings here—that is, beings whose powers are limited. The *infinite* and *perfect* being must be treated altogether differently from His creations, the finite beings, even though we may think of Him as a *feeling being* possessing *supreme blessedness*.

We are certainly correct when we conceive of *God's blessedness* as an unchanging, self-contained blessedness grounded in its consciousness of itself, such that we can find nothing *outside it* that would augment or diminish it. Our limited powers, by contrast, can be augmented or diminished. Now, I claim that the *augmentation* of our powers is experienced as *delight* and that their *diminution* is experienced as pain. Let us consider the fact that simply *becoming conscious* of a power or ability to effect something is in itself a form of this power's augmentation, particularly because it puts us in the position of being able to make an efficient use of it. From this consideration it clearly follows that everything that makes us *acquainted* with our powers is pleasant and agreeable—for example, when we become conscious of having *effected* something by them. The more noble and important a power is, the more delight we derive from its augmentation, even if we are not conscious of this increase; this is all the more true when we are conscious of it. We experience pleasure whenever we exert our powers in a way that is not too easy but also not so difficult that our other powers are diminished. In particular, rigorous, but not too rigorous, meditation brings us pleasure, especially when all of our cognitive powers are set in motion, and even more so when our success in drawing a correct inference shows us that we have not made a false judgment. Such meditation brings us even greater pleasure when it does not demand that we be distinctly conscious of every single thought involved—that is, when our thoughts proceed with such ease and swiftness that we are unable to say how we made the right inference, even though we have clearly done so. Given the fact that there are certain events that bring us delight and pleasure, it is obvious that everything that serves as a *means* to their actualization, and even everything that serves as a *sign* of their approach, also brings us pleasure. Finally, we can rejoice from every form of ethical good brought about by ourselves or others, and even from every object that facilitates the actualization of ethical aims, but only on the condition that the commandments of duty have become the rules guiding our actions, that we live with the conviction that every avoidance of our duty only does us harm and brings us no good, and that we are conscious of the universal truth that the happiness of all increases correlatively with the sacredness of the world's ethical laws and principles.

10

But enough of these general remarks. Let us begin to apply them to our current task. We have taken it upon ourselves to uncover the *source* of our pleasure in the beautiful. A starting point for our inquiry is the fact that only *human beings* with more or less developed cognitive powers are able to experience this pleasure, *animals* being wholly *incapable* of it, *higher beings* transcending it. The first thing apparent to us is the fact that our pleasure in the beautiful does not originate in the *thought of the possible benefits* that the beautiful object might bring us or others, however important these benefits might be. Although it is true that the consideration of the possible benefits to be derived from an object might cause us to take pleasure in the object, this cannot hold for the specific sort of pleasure that we experience when contemplating beautiful objects. This is proven by the impossibility of explaining how we came to doubt that higher beings can experience pleasure in the beautiful, because we normally think of higher beings—at least those with good intentions—as beings who take pleasure in everything that is good and beneficent, if not for themselves, then at least for others. How, then, could they possibly view the beautiful with indifference, if it is something beneficial to us? Would not their pleasure in the beautiful necessarily stand in direct correlation to the clarity and distinctness of their perception of its capacity to be truly beneficial to us? Such an understanding of the nature of the beautiful and the origin of the pleasure we experience in contemplating it is also refuted by our innermost feelings. If the representation of the object's utility for ourselves or for others were the cause of our pleasure, would we not have to be in a position to rigorously meditate on the nature of this utility, clearly articulating its purpose? But we are incapable of doing such a thing. There are thousands of objects that we find beautiful and observe with the greatest pleasure without being able to identify a single benefit that comes to us or to others from them, no matter how long we might have thought about our preference for them. Everybody finds rainbows beautiful without being able to derive any use from them; everybody finds the sight of wildflowers more beautiful than that of wheat fields, even though the former are of no use to us and the latter are of the greatest use; we view the uncaged tiger with fear, whereas we contemplate the beauty of the caged tiger with the greatest pleasure. So, if the pleasure we experience in the beautiful object does not lie in the utility it has for us, then what does it lie in? If it is not to be found in the features of the object revealed by our contemplation, then it must be found in the *activity of contemplation itself*—that is, in the way the object occasions our cognitive powers to *engage* with it. If neither creatures with lesser capacities nor spirits with greater capacities than ours are able to experience pleasure in the beautiful, then such pleasure must clearly be conditioned by a relation *our* cognitive powers have to the object. Our pleasure derives from the fact that the object gives our powers an occasion to contemplate it in a way that is neither too easy nor too difficult for them. Such commensurability with our powers spurs their *growth*. We experience this growth of our powers even when we are not distinctly conscious of it, simply feeling it with pleasure, and this feeling of pleasure is itself the pleasure that we take when contemplating the beautiful. In an hour when we are not bothered by any pressing needs, our eye (mental or physical) is confronted with an object the very representation of which catches our attention and invites us to further contemplation. We find before us a number of features that cannot be readily deduced from one another. We immediately decide to form an exhaustive concept of this object (even if we do not consciously form this decision or do not explicitly state it to ourselves). This excites our imagination in the liveliest way, and at the same moment we imagine the features of objects similar to the contemplated object, but which the contemplated object itself lacks. Using our power of judgment and our powers of reason, we make an appropriate selection of features of the other objects that might also be shared with the object in question. In combining them with those qualities of the object that our perception has revealed to us, we produce a concept of it. We put this concept's adequacy to the test by continuing to contemplate the object. The correctness of our concept is proven if it corresponds to the object itself—that is, if our continued observation reveals that the features we had presumed to be there from the outset are indeed actual features of the object or if our observation at least reveals that the object's actual qualities can be deduced from our concept. At this moment, our cognitive powers are *augmented*, because the correctness of their method has been confirmed. Thus, it is no wonder that we experience a singular pleasure at the end of our contemplation. But if our pleasure in the beautiful is not distinguished by anything more than the fact that it is an activity that *exercises* and *augments* our cognitive powers, then it is ultimately of the same nature as the pleasure we experience when our method of inquiry is proven correct by its end result—for instance, when we complete a *mathematical proof.* But, in all actuality, there lies a great difference between these two forms of pleasure. And although most people are receptive to the pleasure afforded by the contemplation of the beautiful, few have mental powers that are developed enough to enable them to feel pleasure in mathematical proofs and true speculation.[16] Why? Engaging in mathematical or speculative inquiries is

---

16. I purposely say *true* speculation, by which I mean speculation in which we strive to maintain a clear and distinct consciousness of the contents and foundations of every single one of the thoughts involved. This is certainly necessary in mathematical inquiries, but is even more so in those of philosophy if we are to avoid drawing illusory and false conclusions. In my opinion, there are two causes of error in that division of philosophy whose theories are based not on experience but on reason alone: lack of clear and distinct concepts or (in rare cases even combined with) a passion that obscures judgment. Even if it seems clear to me that one does not usually do anything more to clarify one's concepts than the love of truth demands, such that one not fall into error, and even if I am of the opinion that nobody has yet clearly conceptualized what *true clarity and distinctness is and what it demands,* I nevertheless claim that the philosophy of our time, and precisely the philosophy that claims to be the only justified philosophy, has neglected its duty to be clear and distinct in a heretofore unheard of degree and has even refused to acknowledge this duty. How this has come to pass, I do not know—whether it simply be caused by disgust with the tasteless and superfluous way *Wolff* and others used to believe they were fulfilling this duty, I do not wish to investigate. However, the fact that it is so is, I think, obvious. Can one at all deny that our modern philosophers use the words and expressions central to their systems in such ambiguous, unclear, indeterminate ways that confusion about their meaning could never be greater? To name some examples: the absolute, the identity of difference, certainty and truth, concept and object, representation and idea, judgment and syllogism, negation, sublation, relation, contradiction, possibility, actuality and necessity, finite and infinite, essence, substance, personality, freedom, eternity, and so forth. Can one deny that one blames the other for having misunderstood them and that, at the same time, nobody bothers to *clarify* what they mean by certain words, not to speak of listing the constituents of the concept that they want to signify with them? But most decisive is the fact that the history of philosophy gives us an example of a man who lacked the

entirely different from losing oneself in the contemplation of a beautiful object. With the former, we take care to develop all of our thoughts *as distinctly as possible*, clearly conscious of our movement from one concept, proposition, or inference to the next. With the latter, however, we are not at all concerned with becoming distinctly conscious of our thoughts. Rather, we hurry as quickly as possible from one thought to another until we have come across a concept that represents the object in such a way that it contains the sum of the qualities that our contemplation has revealed to us. Thus, in the former case, our ability to think *clearly and distinctly* is exercised and augmented, whereas, in the latter, our ability to think by means of *obscure representations* is exercised and augmented. It is therefore completely understandable that the pleasure we experience in the first case is of a wholly different nature from the pleasure we experience in the second. It is no wonder that we experience pleasure when we are given the occasion to augment our ability to draw correct inferences by means of obscure representations, or even when we have an inkling that this ability is being augmented, because, although it is easier, it is of no less value, and it is actually more useful

---

gift of clear thought to such a degree that he—it can be proven—could not understand the simplest mathematical proofs, despite having, he admits, spent twenty-five years with them and, nevertheless, was able to attain such prominence in the field of philosophy that we now all know the name of *G. W. F. Hegel*! Would you not believe it to be a marvel more stupendous than any *Strauss* ever dealt with when you hear of men who can hardly get a grasp of their own thoughts and who nevertheless claim to be in possession of a philosophical system that is supposed to be "the truth and the whole truth," even "*the truth fully transparent to itself*"? — No, I say, the abstractions of philosophy are infinitely more difficult than those of mathematics, and whoever is incapable of understanding the figures and symbolic constructions of mathematics, incapable of applying the general formula to the individual problem and keeping error at bay, that person should not even attempt to hold discussions in the field of philosophy. In this academic discipline one will get nowhere, or, to use Kant's expression, one will not be able to get on their feet, unless they are absolutely resolved to precisely *understand* the meaning of each of their expressions. Moreover, they will not be able to get on their feet, unless they do not shy away from demonstrating whether the concepts signified by these expressions are *simple* or *complex* and, if the latter, do not shy away from determining the concepts of which they are composed. This seemingly indifferent investigation leads to the most astonishing results and is capable of deciding disputes that would have otherwise lasted an eternity.

for everyday life. This, indeed, is the pleasure we experience when we contemplate a beautiful object and attempt to develop a concept of its beauty. In essence, it is a pleasure in our *contemplation itself.* Without the object, however, we would have no occasion for this contemplation. We therefore necessarily *project* our pleasure onto the object, all the more so because we can only feel the augmentation of our cognitive capacity: we cannot be distinctly conscious of it, cannot *represent* it, and therefore cannot make a *judgment* about it. If this explication of our pleasure in the beautiful is correct, then we have a remarkable example of how human beings are capable of deriving correct conclusions from obscure premises: the pleasure afforded us by the beautiful is a pleasure that cannot be shared by higher or lower beings, even though we cannot explain whence this pleasure arises in a distinct manner. But the reason for this judgment is now clear: animals are incapable of engaging in the sort of contemplation dealt with here, and higher spirits are incapable of augmenting and strengthening their powers by such contemplation, and therefore they cannot experience the same pleasure as human beings do when engaging in it.

11

By answering the second question posed in §6, we have become acquainted with a second, very complex attribute of the beautiful: *the beautiful must be an object whose contemplation can cause pleasure in all people whose cognitive powers are duly developed. This pleasure occurs because, after apprehending some of the object's qualities, the formation of a concept of the object is neither too easy nor too difficult and does not occasion the rigor of distinct thought. Moreover, the pleasure occurs because the concept thus formed, in making it possible to guess at those qualities of the object only accessible to further contemplation, affords at least an obscure awareness of the proficiency of one's cognitive powers.* Since the correct apprehension of this attribute is of central importance for our concept (that is, that pleasure in the beautiful indeed arises in the way outlined here), it is not superfluous to add a few remarks. My readers would most directly convince themselves of the correctness of this explication if they were

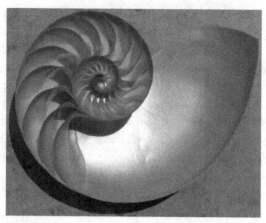

Figure 4

to engage in intense introspection while contemplating a beautiful object, thus becoming *distinctly conscious* of the fact that they do indeed experience thoughts like the ones described here. But as it is certainly easier to form a distinct awareness of our mental processes after someone else has said something about them, I would like to give some examples of beautiful objects, outlining the thought processes involved in their observation and contemplation. If someone asks us if we find a fairly precisely drawn logarithmic spiral—the curve of which moves at a forty-five-degree angle—to be beautiful, we will certainly state, after a moment's contemplation, that we do indeed find it pleasing. What have we engaged with here, and what affords us this gratification? Like any other object that we contemplate with leisure, the drawing would occasion us to ask: what sort of object is this? Under what concept can it be subsumed? And we are certainly capable of giving an answer. We immediately perceived that the line before us has two characteristics: one of its segments progressively approaches a certain point (namely, the midpoint of the spiral), whereas the other gets progressively farther and farther away from this point. We realized that, in order to form a concept of this line, we have to understand the law that dictates that the line approaches the midpoint on the one hand and moves away from it on the other. Soon thereafter, we hit upon the idea that this law might indeed be that of *congruence*—that is, that an angle's distance from the midpoint increases at a constant rate or, alternatively, that this distance increases according to a set ratio. Contemplating further, we find our conjecture confirmed: as far as the naked eye can see, the distance from the midpoint is doubled with every curve. We perceive this without having to undertake any sort of measurement, without having to have a distinct consciousness of this law in our mind, and without even having to articulate our thought in words. This pleases us, and that is why we call the line beautiful. We read a literary work for the first time in our lives, say, the fable "The Wolf and the Lamb."[17] After reading a few lines, we already have an idea of who the wolf and the lamb are supposed to represent, and we can guess how the story is going to turn out. Reading further, we find our conjectures confirmed. Similarly, we find that the new conjectures we developed while reading about the wolf's constant accusations are also confirmed. When we consider the entire story after having read it, we find that every single word served to further the author's purpose—namely, to express the *lesson* that we had anticipated the whole time and that was fully articulated at the end of the story. The fact that we are capable of anticipating the lesson while reading the story and understanding the lesson at the story's conclusion, and the fact that we are able to do so with ease and with such speed that we have no need of being distinctly conscious of all the individual thoughts involved, delights us by demonstrating the proficiency of our cognitive capacities. For this reason, we call the story beautiful. Finally, we are given a *riddle*. After pondering it for some time, we should be able to find its solution. Solving the riddle should not be so easy that anyone can do it, nor should it be so difficult that it can only be done by chance. Rather, we should be able to find the solution by eliminating possible choices by ratiocination. But we should also be able to do this all in a matter of seconds, without wrapping ourselves up in strenuous thought; we should be able to do it without being distinctly conscious of all the inferences we have to make in order to eliminate the wrong choices. And after we have found the solution, it should become clear to us at once why the riddle's author formulated it in the way he did and not in any other. We will take pleasure in the riddle because it will have demonstrated our ability to make a well

---

17. ["The Wolf and the Lamb" is Aesop's fable number 155, and fable 1.10 in the collection by Jean de la Fontaine.]

thought-out guess and because our power of judgment will have profited from the exercise. We will therefore call it a *beautiful* riddle.

12

I believe that I can substantiate the correctness of my explication in §11 of the origins of our liking for the beautiful with a few more arguments. Admittedly, I will not offer arguments with clear-cut conclusions, but I will nevertheless give arguments that cannot be contested in the same way that the appeals to individual feelings in the previous section might be. My *first* argument is that our pleasure in the beautiful cannot be grounded in anything other than the reasons I have given, because there are countless cases *where there is no other conceivable explanation of the origins of the pleasure*. To convince ourselves of this fact, we need only take into account the examples given in the previous section. If the undeniable pleasure we experience when contemplating a spiral or some other geometrical figure does not have its origin in the sources I have elucidated, then I challenge anyone to give a better explanation. This pleasure cannot have its origins in the thought of the possible utility that such geometrical figures might have or in their similarity with some valuable object. In the end, there is really no other feasible explanation than the one given. Will anyone have more success in explaining the pleasure we find in the fable "The Wolf and the Lamb"? Is not the beauty of the fable diminished the moment we admit that one of its parts seems to us to lack purpose? Finally, it is clear that nothing else can cause our pleasure in solving the beautiful riddle but our awareness of the proficiency of our powers of thinking and guessing.

13

The *second* argument I bring in to support the correctness of my explication is the following: *the degree of pleasure we experience when contemplating a beautiful object increases in correlation with the proficiency that we demonstrate in our apprehension of it or with the way the object exercises and makes demands of our cognitive powers.* So, for example, even a simple chord (say a note and its octave) played over a long duration can please us. This is because even being able to hear the chord correctly (namely, as a chord made up of a note and its octave) and identify it demands training. Our pleasure is undeniably greater when we hear more complex chords, such as triads, and it increases when we are capable of naming the notes of the chord. Why? Clearly because distinguishing the notes of a triad demands more practice and skill. To give another example that will make this point even more clear, we no doubt experience more pleasure when looking at the outline of a beautiful palace or temple than we do when simply looking at one of its parts—a gate, for instance. Similarly, nobody will question the fact that a riddle appears all the more beautiful the more we are able to demonstrate our wit in solving it. Our views on the pleasure derived from contemplating the beautiful are thus certainly not wrong, because they are able to account for its varying degrees and types.

14

Having set aside all doubt concerning the attribute of the beautiful explicated in §11, we are now in the position of being able to see whether we can develop a concept that, if not identical with the concept of the beautiful, is at least of the same extension. We need not worry about the extension of the concept being too *narrow*, because the fact that each one of the attributes explicated up to now (in §§3, 5, 6, 7, 10) is *general* means that even if we bring *all* of these attributes together we will still end up with a concept applicable to every beautiful object. Conversely, though, such a concept could run the danger of being redundant. If the features implied by one of its constituents are already implied by one or more of its other constituents, then the former could be left out without expanding the concept's extension. This would certainly occur if we were to add any of the attributes we explicated earlier to the one explicated in §11, because the latter contains all of the former, either directly as constituents or indirectly by inference. Let us recall our explication of *the beautiful as an object whose contemplation can cause pleasure in all people whose cognitive powers are duly developed*. *This pleasure occurs because, after apprehending some of the object's qualities, the formation of a concept of the object is neither too easy nor too difficult and does not occasion the rigor of distinct thought. Moreover, the pleasure occurs because the concept thus formed, in making it possible to guess at those qualities of the object only accessible to further contemplation, affords at least an obscure awareness of the proficiency of one's cognitive powers*. This explication contains the *first* attribute, developed in §3, that the beautiful object is one that *is capable of pleasing us by its mere contemplation*. Further, this explication contains the *second* attribute, developed in §5, that the contemplation by which the beautiful object is able to please us must proceed *with such ease and swiftness that we need not be distinctly conscious of all the thoughts involved*. Finally, although this explication does not explicitly contain the *third* attribute, developed in §6, it does imply that our mind *may not simply be concerned with the particular relation the object has to us as individuals*. After all, the beautiful cannot have its source in the object's exclusive relation to us as individuals if every other person with duly developed cognitive powers must be in a position of being able to form a concept of it in the way explained in §5 and thus can derive the same pleasure from it. Moreover, all the other aspects of the beautiful described in §6 can be found in this explication. Judgments of beauty have a certain claim to *universal validity*, namely that every person who is duly trained in their powers, especially in their powers of cognition, can enjoy objects that we judge to be beautiful. *Animals* and as yet uneducated *children* are held not to have a sense of the beautiful. And, finally, spirits of a higher kind than ourselves are admitted to have *knowledge* of the beautiful but experience no *enjoyment* in its contemplation. Similarly, every aspect of our meditation on the content of the contemplation of the beautiful (§7) is either explicitly contained in the explication or is implied in such a way as to make any dispute about it superfluous.

Do the attributes of the beautiful explicated [in §11] make all these others superfluous? Do we have to hold on to all of them? Can we not omit one or more without expanding the concept's extension? It might appear that we can do without the idea that the contemplation of the beautiful must bring about our *pleasure*, and we can do without the idea that this pleasure must have its roots in the way this contemplation makes it *possible for us to have at least an obscure awareness of the proficiency of our own cognitive powers*, because both of these ideas can be readily deduced from the remaining characteristics of the contemplation outlined in the given explication. Let us recall that our explication states that the beautiful object is such that forming a concept of it must be neither too easy nor too difficult for the person whose cognitive powers are duly developed. It must thus be possible for them to guess at those qualities of the object that are not readily apparent to their apprehension and can only be revealed by further contemplation. Does it not follow from this that the object makes it possible for them to at least have an obscure awareness of the proficiency of their own cognitive powers? And, further, does it not follow from this again that the contemplation of such an object must give them pleasure? This is true in most cases, but not all. For example, if we see somebody with an expression of despair running up and down the shore of a raging river and then stopping at the deepest point, we feel anxiety because we think that this person is contemplating suicide. When, indeed, he throws himself into the river, do we call this sight *beautiful*? Even though our correct anticipation has actually proven the proficiency of our cognitive powers, the event is so awful that nobody would, at that moment, venture to think about the proficiency of their cognitive powers and rejoice in it. We therefore neither have an obscure awareness of nor derive pleasure from the proficiency of our cognitive powers every time they are exercised in a way that is not too easy or too difficult. And only when the object of our contemplation is capable of giving us such pleasure do we claim that it is truly beautiful.

15

Thus, every aspect of the explication of the beautiful recapitulated at the beginning of the previous section is essential; none of them can be omitted without altering the concept itself. Nevertheless, we must ask ourselves whether something must still be added to this explication in order for it to adequately describe the concept designated by the word "beautiful" (or at least a concept wholly equivalent to it). Is not our explication of the concept of the *beautiful* still too broad? If this is the case, then we must ensure that our explication has the proper extension by *limiting* it in some way. But how should we go about doing this? Should we limit the *type* of object capable of occasioning the sort of contemplation outlined in our explication? Maybe we could claim that it is only one *particular sort of object*—those that can be apprehended by our senses perhaps? But our everyday language also allows and even demands that we call some *super-sensory* objects beautiful: do we not often speak of a *beautiful soul*? *Virtue*, something that certainly is not tangible to our senses, has since ancient times been called beautiful, indeed most beautiful. The same goes for *holy spirits* and even *godliness* itself. Or should we give a more precise determination of the *type of pleasure* occasioned by the beautiful object—or maybe of its origins? But how should we limit this part of our explication? It already excludes so many things, either in itself or by inferences that can easily be drawn from it: it excludes everything that is merely *gratifying to our senses*, everything that only pleases us by virtue of its particular relation to *us as individuals* as well as everything that pleases us simply by virtue of its *usefulness*. Similarly, our explication makes clear that the beautiful only provides us with mental pleasure, arising from our discovery of a rule from which we are able to derive all the qualities to be apprehended in the beautiful object. The discovery of this rule must be neither too easy nor too difficult so that we need not be distinctly conscious of every single thought involved in it. How could we possibly limit our concept any further? Nobody could seriously demand that we limit in advance the *number* of discrete features that are needed to form our concept of it or that we can deduce from the concept already formed. Nor could anybody seriously ask us to determine the *intensity of the pleasure* occasioned by the contemplation of a beautiful object. As our explication leaves it undetermined, we might be led to presume that there are different *degrees of beauty*. Or should we further qualify the being capable of enjoying the beautiful? We claimed that this being must be *a human being whose powers, especially their cognitive powers, are duly developed*. From this it follows that their liking for the object is not merely a product of their personal flaws or foibles. I do not think that one can really develop this part of our explication any further. But even if our explication expands the meaning of the beautiful, this would certainly not be a bad thing if our concept had some significance of its own, which, it is hoped, will not be denied. Is it not certain that the type of object we have explicated deserves its own *name* either way? There is a type of object that pleases every person whose cognitive powers are duly developed, increasing their awareness of the proficiency of their capacity to think by means of obscure representations. Should we not use such objects to relax after a long day's work? Or to increase our enjoyment of life? More importantly, should we not give young people plenty of opportunity to interact with such objects? In developing a taste for such objects, young people would not only develop their cognitive powers but would also be able to help their own communities grasp the most important truths and convictions. And if we did not already have a name for objects of this sort, which word could possibly be more appropriate than the word "beautiful"? I think that the explication given in §14 really captures the way this word is used and that it is at least a concept *equivalent* to the one aestheticians have for centuries denoted by the word "beautiful," if it is not the same concept. Why do I not say that it is the *same* concept? How contentious that would be! Because who is in a position to say what other people have since their earliest years signified with the word "beautiful"? And who is to say what comes to people's minds when they use the word? Indeed, they might still view these associations as essential parts of the concept's meaning. But that the constituents of the concept given in my explication are not wholly foreign to the concept in question and that they are really contained in most people's understanding of the beautiful is proven by the fact that so many perceptive thinkers have come across the very same constituents in their own attempts to explicate the beautiful, as I will show below.

16

Much of what can be *inferred* from our explication of the beautiful finds its exact counterpart in other works of aesthetics. I take this to be further confirmation of its correctness. I will thus allow myself to list only the most important conclusions here.

1. Our explication is able to account for the fact that we often have a difficult time explaining why we find a certain object beautiful or not, a problem all aestheticians attempt to account for. Some used to think—and some people still do think—that our judgments of taste are made *immediately*, without reference to any concepts or rules, or that they follow from premises that are *inexpressible*. The reason for this is quite natural, however. It results from the fact that the thoughts accompanying our enjoyment of the beautiful are carried out with such ease and swiftness that we hardly become distinctly conscious of them. We usually deem representations and judgments of which we have no distinct consciousness to be *inexpressible*, and sometimes we are even inclined to deny that they exist in our minds at all.

2. Our explication makes it conceivable why only *two* of our senses are capable of bringing us representations of the beautiful—namely, the *higher* senses of *sight* and *hearing*—a fact taught by all scholars of aesthetics [*Ästhetiker*]. The representations given by the *lower* senses of *taste* and *smell* are too simple for a rule to be observed in their composition or succession, the discovery of which would allow us to contemplate them in a way that would be pleasing for our cognitive capacities. For example, would it please us to be able to guess the rule followed by a host who alternates sweet, sour, and salty dishes? Certain objects perceived by our sense of touch, certain plastic objects, can in some cases, such as when a trained eye looks over them, reveal to us relations varied and yet rule-guided enough to please us. But this would almost certainly proceed too slowly for us to be able to derive the singular sort of pleasure afforded us by the contemplation of the beautiful.

3. Our explication makes it perfectly conceivable why an object that is supposed to afford us full enjoyment of the beautiful must be wholly new to us, or have some features that are new to us, or features that we previously overlooked. Only then does the contemplation of the object make us exert our cognitive powers in the necessary way. Complex objects with many distinct parts, such as paintings or long poems, can be exhaustively comprehended only by the most varied contemplation. Thus, the pleasure they afford us grows with repeated contemplation over time, whereas things whose beauty is of a simpler nature soon sate our interest.

4. Our explication also makes it clear why different stages of cognitive development demand different objects if the person contemplating the object is to take delight in it and do more than coldly admit that it is beautiful. The simplest beauties are enough for children and savages; they are unable to grasp more complex ones.[18] By contrast, people who have developed their tastes in many ways do not deny that such simple objects are beautiful, even if this beauty is of a lesser sort. But they do not rejoice in them. They only derive enjoyment from something *higher*, from more complex objects, those whose organizational principles are not so uniform and not easily understood.

17

I am not entirely certain whether the following will be counted among those things that confirm the correctness of my explication of the beautiful, because I am not sure whether it will be admitted that this inference has already been drawn by others. It follows from my explication that only some select objects are capable of occasioning a *pure* pleasure in the beautiful not mixed with any other sensation. That is because, following from my explication, practically only *pictures* (spatial relations) and *sound sequences of varying duration* (temporal relations) are capable of causing such a pleasure. The pleasure we experience when contemplating other types of beautiful objects is usually augmented by some other sort of pleasure. Along with their beauty, they are *gratifying* to our senses in some other way, or they please us by opening the prospect of some other form of *enjoyment*, or we derive pleasure from contemplating their integral *design*, their high degree of *utility* for us or for others, or their inner value, their *ethical goodness and excellence*: all of these objects bring us pleasure of a wholly different sort from the pleasure that is derived from contemplating them and forming

---

18. [The word here translated as "savages" is *"Wilden,"* which is cognate with "wild" in English and which was standardly used at the time to refer to Indigenous peoples. So used, it was often derogatory. In his ethical and political writings, Bolzano insists that all human beings are owed equal consideration (2007 *passim*).]

an exhaustive concept of them. However much these merits might increase our pleasure in some objects, we cannot allow them to tip the scale of our judgments regarding the objects' *degree of beauty*. The only thing of relevance when considering the *true beauty* of an object is the degree to which its contemplation can please us without requiring the effort of distinct thought. The ways they might please us beyond this are not the object of this essay. To give a few examples: when judging the beauty of a piece of *music*, the pleasures caused by the sensations and moods associated with the sound of the *instruments* or the sound of the *human voice* should not come into consideration (though they tend to affect us in an almost magical way). Rather, it is only the *appropriate arrangement and selection* of these instruments that is essential to the music's beauty, because it is the aspect that a practiced and knowledgeable listener can at least obscurely discern. Thus, every song performed by a voice that is gratifying to the senses—for instance, by a soothing voice—has a *mixed beauty*. This is also true of every *poem* that makes us *enthusiastic* about something, that fills our breast with great feeling and determination, feelings we experience with pleasure. The beauty of the *human form* is a very mixed kind of beauty. In addition to those things that the explication of the beautiful developed here compels us to find beautiful, there is a whole plethora of representations caused by the sight of a beautiful person that *can* and sometimes *should* be pleasurable to us. Does it not belong to the essential characteristics of the human body that we see not only the person's physical but also their spiritual health, that we see in the person's face both understanding and judgment, goodness and kindness? Can we refrain from sensing our own pleasure at the sight of such perfections?

18

We usually maintain that the *ugly* is the opposite of the beautiful, although it might be more precise, though a little less conventional, to say the *foul*. So, if our explication of the beautiful is correct, then we must be in a position to explicate the concept of the *ugly* in a way that makes it clear why it is the opposite of the beautiful. Indeed, this should pose no problem for us. Let us first recall our explication of the beautiful as an object whose contemplation can cause pleasure in all people whose cognitive powers are duly developed; a pleasure that occurs because, after apprehending some of the object's qualities, the formation of a concept of the object is neither too easy nor too difficult and it does not occasion the rigor of distinct thought; finally, a pleasure that results from the fact that the concept thus formed, in making it possible to guess at those qualities of the object only accessible to further contemplation, affords at least an obscure awareness of the proficiency of one's cognitive powers. By contrast, the *ugly is an object that vexes us, at least when we do not make the effort to maintain the rigor of clear and distinct thought: it vexes us because every time we apprehend the object's qualities and attempt to develop a concept of it, we always find something that contradicts the concept that we have formed of it.* A few examples will serve to convince us that this explication is not false. In a poem that otherwise follows a specific rhyme scheme, we find it ugly when a rhyme is suddenly missing or out of place. Why? For the simple reason that the presence of a rhyme scheme throughout the poem has led us to expect—and justified the expectation—that the rhyme scheme will be maintained in the rest of the poem: we are vexed the moment this legitimate expectation is dashed. Similarly, when the structure and parts of a building lead us to believe that it is constructed according to principles of symmetry, we are vexed when we come upon a part that deviates from this principle. Our vexation is not diminished if somebody then attempts to demonstrate to us by precise measurements that the deviation is only apparent, that it is indeed balanced out by other parts of the building that are hardly perceptible to us: the notion that such measurements should be at all necessary in itself contradicts what it means to be beautiful. This not only shows that the ugly in and of itself is capable of vexing us and is thus the opposite of the beautiful. From this it also follows that there is a *mixed ugliness* in cases where the object is also displeasing to our senses, just as there is a *mixed beauty* in cases where the object is also gratifying to our senses. This also makes it clear why we can perceive *ugly things* within a *beautiful whole* with pleasure, as when an ugly person appears at the right place and the right time in a comedy. If they are integrated into the beautiful whole in such a way that it corresponds to a formal rule that we have deduced

from the comedy's structure, then these otherwise ugly beings may
be regarded with pleasure and considered to be *beautiful in relation to
the whole.*

19

In order to avoid giving the impression that I am keeping anything
from the reader that might be of relevance in making a judgment about
the correctness of my explication, I would like to consider *some objections
that might be made against it.* I will state with honesty what I consider
the most important objections, and I will attempt to counter them. But
I will not consider the case closed until I have expounded on some of
the most noteworthy explications others have given and until I have
explained why I have been unable to remain satisfied with any of them.[19]
   1. First and foremost, one might object that there are objects
wholly lacking in complexity and a multitude of distinct parts that
we can nevertheless find beautiful, such as simple colors or sounds.
This would then show that my explication of the origins of the pleasure in the beautiful is incorrect. Or are there cases where, when contemplating a simple color and attempting to answer the question of
what color it is, our cognitive powers are activated in such a way as
to give us an awareness of their proficiency? It must be remembered
that it has yet to be decided whether objects of such simplicity may be
called *beautiful* in the true sense of the word or are simply *gratifying to
our senses.* The answer ultimately depends on a few things: it depends
on whether our contemplation of single sounds and colors consists in
anything more than merely *perceiving* them with our senses (which
animals are capable of doing too), whether contemplating these simple
objects demands the sort of proficiency of mind developed by lengthy
practice, and whether we exert, if not all, then at least most of our cognitive powers when contemplating them. Whoever thinks that each
of these should be answered in the negative will certainly also deny
that colors and sounds have a beauty of their own, and, in so doing,

---

19. [Here Bolzano refers to §§26–57, not included in this translation.]

they will prove that they make this judgment in a way wholly in line with my concept of the beautiful. But with time I have come to believe that all of those things are indeed true. A color evenly spread over a surface, a pure tone sounded in a steady diminuendo: these too are complex objects with a multitude of distinct parts that must be taken up in contemplation. If we are to experience *pleasure* in the pure tone and its duration, then we must know that the duration of the vibrations caused in our ears by the displacement of the ether or air has a certain magnitude or, further, that the duration of the *alterations* caused in our *mind itself* by these nervous vibrations has itself a certain magnitude. Experience teaches us that making such precise observations is not an easy task and requires practice. Furthermore, whoever has a mind keen enough to make such observations will find it necessary to contemplate the sounds and colors and sense their beauty over a longer period of time—that is, they will be compelled to *lose themselves* in them. Finally, it is clear that such observation requires not only the exertion of our capacities of sensuous perception but also the exertion of our memory, imagination, and power of judgment. For all these reasons, it is clear that the pleasure we experience when contemplating such objects is a pleasure in the *beautiful* in the precise sense explicated here. It is certainly true that we can refine our *sense of taste* by practice, which is shown by the example of cooks and gourmets who are capable of telling us the ingredients in a dish just by tasting it, often with more precision than a chemical analysis. But now somebody might want to infer from what I have said here that people of this kind experience the pleasures of their refined taste as *beautiful* pleasures. In my explication of the beautiful object, however, I claim that the gratification afforded to us by contemplating the object is not derived from those features readily apparent to our perception. Rather, I claim that our gratification is derived from correctly *guessing* the presence of certain aspects of the object wholly *independent* of those features that can be inferred from those we can perceive but that are nevertheless related to them in a way essential to the composition of the object as a whole. Do we encounter anything of the kind when the gourmet tells us the vintage and the origin of the wine he is drinking? Or when he lists off all the spices and other ingredients in the dish he just ate? He does not make a *guess* as to the other ingredients a dish might contain on the

basis of the flavors he has already tasted. Rather, he infers the presence
of other ingredients that have a *necessary* connection with those he has
already tasted in the dish. But things are completely different when we
listen to a sound, even if only a single one. As soon as the sound's first
vibrations reach our ear, we listen for how *high* the note is; that is, we
attempt to discern the relation between the duration of the vibrations
and some length of time that we are familiar with and that we consider
to be unalterable (namely, that of a particular mental activity, such as
counting). If we practice enough and if the sound is indeed a pure
tone, then the attempt is not likely to fail. Nevertheless, we will not be
distinctly conscious of what note it is; rather, it will simply come to us.
After having identified the sound, we will then see whether the next
sound in the sequence is identical to it. If it turns out to be so, thus
confirming that our initial guess was correct, then everything essential
to pleasure in the beautiful is present. Nevertheless, I admit that the
pleasure afforded to us by a *single* sound or a *single* color is slight and
that such objects must have a *low* degree of beauty. Only when we are
given a sequence of multiple sounds or colors ordered in a specific way
whose law is not all too easily (but also not too difficultly) guessed
at will we experience a higher pleasure. And the whole sequence will
undoubtedly deserve to be called *beautiful*.

20

2. On the one hand, there are objects that can be apprehended *all too
easily* for them to deserve to be called *beautiful*. On the other hand, it
will be said, there are objects the apprehension of which demands *far
too much exertion* on our part for them to be called *beautiful* according
to my explication. How much study is demanded to properly interpret
the meaning of a poem written in an ancient language, a poem that
we call beautiful, even though the attempt to apprehend it has made
us exert our minds to the fullest, maybe even more than attempting to
apprehend the most difficult of Euclid's theorems might have! I reply:
when we call a poem—or any other object for that matter—beautiful,
we do not claim that every mode of contemplating it can be pleasing

to us, but only *certain* ones. We do not wish to deny the fact that we often have to arduously examine an object before its contemplation affords us any pleasure. Such arduous examination might entail that we make clear formulations about the object and its contents. However, it is sufficient that our final contemplation of it is such that it can proceed by means of obscure representations and that the content of this contemplation is the same as that indicated in my explication. By contrast, even if we repeat a mathematical demonstration such that we have no need to form a distinct consciousness of its individual parts to ourselves when executing it, we still have no right to speak of beauty, because we do not make any *guesses* but merely *inferences*. The mathematical demonstration is not an object whose manifold features lead us to attempt to formulate a concept of it. Rather, we draw conclusions from it that follow with absolute necessity.

21

3. Another objection might be that my explication equates the beautiful with the *regular* and that there are many things that have a certain regularity that, nevertheless, are by no means beautiful. An example might be a well-made clock. All the same, not everything beautiful must have regularity—as we know, one speaks of *irregular beauty*. According to my explication, however, not every instance of regularity is sufficient for beauty, but only the instances of regularity that can be divined without the effort of clear and distinct thought. And I think that the regularity of an object may only be called beautiful when the contemplation of it contributes to the growth of our cognitive powers. For this it is immediately clear both that there are things with regularity that nobody finds beautiful, such as the functioning of a machine, which can only be understood after arduous analysis, and that there are also beautiful things that lack a *certain* regularity. Even an irregularity—namely, a deviation from a rule that the genus of the object permits us to expect from it—must not necessarily detract from the beauty of an object or destroy its otherwise regular form. Such is the case when we speak of *irregular beauty*. In addition, something that is irregular in one respect

might indeed fit a rule of another sort, so that it might be seen as beautiful. Blushing, stuttering, and awkwardness are doubtless irregular parts of someone's behavior. But in the right circumstances they can have a charming beauty—for instance, when a young woman blushes after her lover has expressed his feelings for her for the first time.

22

4. But one could further object that regularity is not only *not an essential attribute* of the beautiful, but it also detracts from beauty itself. A work of art that we find beautiful must appear to be the product of *free activity*. And a work in which we see the *force of the rules* according to which it was produced must displease us for precisely this reason.

To this I answer that the question of how an object was *produced* is not the question we take up when we want to judge whether that object is beautiful. We do not ask how much exertion the work cost the artist or how many *rules* he followed with painstaking effort: if the work lacks none of the features it should possess, then the way it was produced cannot in any way detract from its beauty. When we look at a beautiful statue, we might think of the fact that sculpting it required much work from the artist, that he had to chisel away at the stone again and again, assisted by his compass and straightedge. But none of this lessens our praise of the statue's beauty. One might say that "one should not be able to see the artist's labor in the work." But if we are to avoid speaking nonsense, what should we understand by this expression? To see the artist's labor in the work can only mean that our observation leads us to surmise from some of its features that its production cost the artist great exertion. Nobody would be so irrational as to criticize the work if it is a *quality beyond reproach* that leads us to suppose that it required great exertion—say, if we think that such a high degree of perfection could only have been obtained by arduous labor. The idea that one should not be able to see the artist's labor in the final product can therefore mean only one thing—namely, that the work should not be able to infer from any *imperfection*—from evidence that the artist deviated from a rule, made a mistake, or overlooked something from fatigue—that the work's production required great exertion. Understood in this sense, my explication of the beautiful raises no objection to the idea that one should not be able to see the artist's labor in the final product. How can it fail to disfigure a work of art when it is readily apparent to us that an artist has insufficiently developed some formal aspect of his work, has deviated from some rule that he himself set, or has even, in consistently developing the formal properties of his work, violated some rule that we hold to be more important than those that he adhered to? These shortcomings are, quite precisely, instances of the *ugly* (see §18). A common example might be a poem whose verse and rhyme scheme are sacrificed for the sake of the ideas and sensations the poet is trying to transmit. Some recent philosophers go even further in claiming that everything beautiful is essentially "irrational." In Weisse's *System of Aesthetics* it is explicitly stated: "a truly speculative science of aesthetics can have no greater task than to destroy at its root the *prejudice* that the key to the concept of beauty is to be found in *rational* proportions."[20] However, in reading the author's "addendum," in which he seeks to "fulfill [this task] to his very best," I have found nothing that even resembles a proof of his claim. Thus, I believe it is reasonable to hold on to this "prejudice," especially because it is verified, as Weisse himself acknowledges, by many examples—for instance, by the fact that melody and harmony in music are dependent upon very *rational*, even *simple, proportions* between sounds and the duration of sounds or by the fact that the dimensions of spatial objects that we find beautiful (including the human body itself) also conform to certain rational proportions. One can only go so far as to say that imperceptibly minute deviations from these rational proportions do not detract from the beauty of the object—for instance, when one foot is slightly shorter than the other. One would not think of treating this as proof of the thesis that such proportions *must necessarily* be irrational. At the most, one can claim that a truly irrational proportion does not detract from the beauty of an object, so long as it is so close to being a rational proportion that we do not perceive it as irrational. In the end, determining whether something is beautiful is not a matter of how the object is, in and of itself, but rather only of how it appears to us.

---

20. [Christian Hermann Weisse, *System der Ästhetik* (Leipzig: Hartmann, 1830): §19.]

23

5. Some might object that my explication of the beautiful implies that an object always increases in beauty the easier and faster all of its features can be guessed from those readily perceivable, so that, for example, a drama whose plot and conclusion we can guess from the very beginning deserves more praise than a more difficult work. This, of course, is not the case. One demands that a play hold us in suspense and keep us guessing until the very last scene. Similarly, *surprises*, plot developments that we could never have foreseen, bring us pleasure, despite the fact that or, even more precisely, because we do not expect them.

That an object appears more beautiful the more easily and more definitively we are able to guess the rest of its features from a few of those that are perceptible is impossible to derive from my explication. Rather, my explication implies that an object's features can be guessed *with too much ease and too definitively*—that is, when the contemplation of the object fails to augment our cognitive powers in any way. There is no way a play or a story could keep our attention if we knew all the details of its plot from the very beginning. This is why it is one of the rules that works of this kind must, to a certain extent, keep us in the dark about the events to come. This, indeed, contributes to the work's beauty. Thus, we find well-placed *surprises* beautiful, especially when the type of plot has led us to suspect that such surprises might come, even though we could never have guessed the particular nature of the surprise itself.

24

6. The ugly is, as I have remarked, the opposite of the beautiful. If my explication of the latter is correct, then my explication of the ugly (§18), which is based on this opposition, must also be correct. But, one might object, my explication of the ugly is clearly mistaken. We call so many things ugly to which this explication does not apply at all! There

are things that offend us in ways quite different from our incapacity to guess their features based on observations of those we perceive. We call *ugly* everything that disgusts us or causes us some other unpleasant sensation, even if only by an association of ideas—for instance, a corpse or a gun that killed a beloved person.

All of this is true. Nevertheless, none of it is really an objection against my explication of the ugly or my explication of the beautiful. Rather, it merely demonstrates that we often use the word "ugly" in a sense in which it is not the exact opposite of the beautiful. We often use it in a sense in which it merely denotes the opposite of the *pleasing in general*. In other cases, we often associate the word "ugly" [*hässlich*] with the word it is derived from, namely "hate" [*Hass*], whereby we think of the ugly as something that is or could be an object of our hatred. In this sense, we might also call things ugly that are nothing less than the opposite of the beautiful and that, despite their ugliness, have many beautiful parts.

25

7. Finally, one might say that the concept of the beautiful is so universal among human beings that it could not possibly be composed of so many parts woven together in a way as artificial as my explication presents it. All peoples, even the least developed [*rohesten*], distinguish between the beautiful and the foul. And however much various judgments concerning the beauty of this or that object might differ from one another, a certain common concept of the beautiful underlies them all. Not only adults but also very young children gradually learn, as they encounter many beautiful objects and many ugly objects, to distinguish between them and to contemplate the beautiful ones with delight. They are aware of the concept of the beautiful. So, the concept must either be simple or, if complex, it must be composed out of a small number of parts related to one another out of a certain inner necessity.

I do not deny that the concept of the beautiful is widespread. But it does not in any way follow that the concept must be composed of very few parts or that it must be a simple concept. Indeed, there are many concepts that are just as widely used, if not more so, and that are, nevertheless, extremely complex. Who would dispute the complexity of the thousands of concepts under which we classify *natural objects* into genera and species? I mean the concepts: horse, dog, cat, bird, fish, tree, shrub, flower, fruit, apple, and so on. Do not even the simplest of these concepts have more parts than the concept of the beautiful as explicated above? And yet how common they are! How quickly every child acquires them! But there really is no great mystery in all of this. The moment multiple objects with similar qualities catch our attention, we attempt to develop a concept that applies to these objects and no others, composing the concept out of the representations we have of those common qualities. We do this in steps, taking constitutive parts into our concept when we perceive that they are common to this type of object, removing them from our concept when we find that they are not universally shared by such objects. And we do all this without being distinctly conscious of doing it; that is, we do not say to ourselves that we are doing it, and, in many cases, we would be incapable of articulating how we developed such a concept. If we want to explain why almost every human being, as soon as they have risen above animal simplicity, has some understanding of the concept of the beautiful, then it suffices to recall that it is an *essential part of our nature as human beings* that once our immediate needs are met, the activity of our restless minds drives us to find an adequate concept for every object we encounter. If we succeed in this with ease and we are even capable of guessing the object's remaining qualities after perceiving only some of them, although the latter might not directly follow from the former, and if we are capable of doing all this without having to form a clear and distinct representation of every single quality, then it is thus understandable that this causes us a certain pleasure. And if we encounter many objects that give us pleasure in this way and if we also encounter others that we have tried in vain to conceptualize in the same way, then it is quite natural that we distinguish the former from the latter, forming the concepts of the beautiful and the ugly. Thus, the origins of these concepts lie in the nature of the human mind. It is no wonder that we find them, developed with varying degrees of distinctness, wherever there are human beings.

On the Classification
of the Fine Arts[1]

1

In the first of these *Essays on Aesthetics*, I found it necessary to discuss
the concept of the *beautiful* in such detail that one might expect that
aesthetics will now amount to little more than a *"theory of the beautiful"*
for me, as it is for most contemporary students of the field. Indeed it
is, in the same way—as I have come to accept—that the explication of
mathematics is the theory of quantities.[2] Just as, in German, one calls
mathematics the *theory of quantities*, one might also call aesthetics the
theory of beauty. At the same time, as with mathematics, further explanation is needed to qualify what is meant by the expression *"theory of
an object."* The expression should not be understood in the strict sense
in which we conceive of the theory of some object—namely, as just a
collection of a number of truths that immediately pertain to the object
or are propositions about it. After all (just speaking of *aesthetics* now,

---

1. [The German is *"Schönen Künste,"* literally the beautiful arts.]

2. In 1810, the author attempted to develop a different explication, one that he is not
ashamed to retract, in his "Contributions to a Better-Grounded Presentation of Mathematics" [Bolzano 2004(1810): 83–137].

because mathematics is of no concern to us here), a study of the components that comprise the *concept* of the beautiful is not, strictly speaking, a proposition about the beautiful itself. Moreover, studies of the sublime, the ridiculous, the humorous, the romantic, the touching, the sentimental, and many other topics that are never left out of treatises on aesthetics cannot be viewed as studies of the beautiful. At least, this is true if one does not want to convince oneself that these are subtypes of the concept of the beautiful and thus fall under its scope. Since this is so clearly an error, it seems sufficient to me simply to mention it here. Even clearer, as long as one does not want to give *"theory of beauty"* a somewhat expanded meaning, we must not pass off as studies in aesthetics those purely historical studies that are found in large quantities in many treatises on aesthetics or in writings considered to be part of the literature on aesthetics—for example, studies on ancient and modern art, on the authenticity of this or that work of art, biographies of artists, and much more.

We have a concept adequate to linguistic usage if we understand *aesthetics* to be a *scientifically organized collection* of all those truths worth knowing that satisfy either one of the two following conditions: They are truths that *immediately concern* the beautiful. Alternatively, they are truths that stand in such a relation to the beautiful that at least one— the truths that immediately concern the beautiful or those that stand in relation to the beautiful—must be properly understood and fruitfully applied in light of the other.

From this follows that:

1. one of the first orders of business in aesthetics must be to inquire into the component parts that constitute the *concept of the beautiful*, which is certainly not a simple concept. Only by developing a precise determination of this concept will we be able to *distinguish* the beautiful from other objects that are similar to it but should not be confused with it. And only then will we be able to correctly name and deduce the general attributes of the beautiful and its various *subtypes*. From this explication it becomes clear

2. why one might view the theory of the *fine arts* as one of the premier components of aesthetics, so much so that some have even gone as far as to conflate aesthetics with the theory of art. The task for a *theory of art* is to state how the most diverse artworks can be produced with

utmost perfection. This aim is, to our mind, one of the highest ends that aesthetics can seek to achieve. After all, there is no more important application of the tenets of the beautiful than teaching artists how they should work to produce art that, while seeming just to afford pleasure, educates thousands of their brothers and wins them over to the good causes of morality and religion. But no matter how highly one might estimate this benefit of a properly designed theory of art, one cannot believe that it alone exhausts *all* the purposes of aesthetics. After all, only some people are destined to become artists, whereas a theory of the beautiful can be useful for everybody if it provides guidance for how we should enjoy every instance of the beautiful that we encounter, not only in *art*, but also in *nature*. In our explication, such guidance will be seen as one of the disciplines of aesthetics. The same holds for more general guidance on the art of living our entire lives as beautifully as possible, enjoying all instances of the beautiful we encounter as much as possible—a doctrine pithily termed *kalobiotics*, or the art of living beautifully.[3]

3. Finally, it has always been recognized that some purely *historical* studies cross over into aesthetics. Our argument justifies situating them in this field, because they can only be interesting and truly useful for people who are familiar with the essence and laws of the beautiful. Examples include accounts of scholars' various opinions and concepts of the beautiful and its laws, accounts of the fate of the arts in various nations in different eras, descriptions of the most remarkable accomplishments in past or contemporary art or artworks, biographies of artists, and much more.

---

3. In 1844, *Wilhelm Bronn* was the first to draw the public's attention to this, until then, disregarded science. See his text, published by Gerold in Vienna, *Für Kalobiotik als neu ausgestecktes Feld menschlichen Strebens* (vol. 1, 1835 and vol. 2, 1838), his book *Kalobiotik, Kunst schön zu leben, wissenschaftlich aufgefasst* (Leipzig: R. Bünder, 1839), and finally, the periodical created by him, *Für Kaliobiotik*, published as a supplement to Rudolf Glaser's journal *Ost und West* (Prague). In doing so, Bronn has performed the service of occasioning some discussion of this important topic.

2

Thus, the *fine arts* are, if not the only, nevertheless one of the most important topics in aesthetics. For this reason, the *concept* of fine art must find its determination in this field of study, as must the concept of a beautiful *work of art*, which is the product brought forth by fine art. Both concepts are completely fixed by linguistic usage. We say that a person possesses beautiful *artistry*, or (what is the same) we call him an *artist*, when he *has the ability to produce, through his free and intentional acts, objects subsumed under the concept of the beautiful in such a way that their beautiful qualities are the result of his technique, which is, in the production of the object, oriented toward this end [of making objects beautiful] and which is thereby conducted in one way and not in any other.* We call these objects themselves (more or less perfect) *works of fine art* or *artworks*. In this explication, acknowledging the *dependency* of the artwork's beautiful features on its producer's particular technique and on his *intentionality* in its technical execution is indispensable if our argument is not to go beyond its limits. For when an apprentice gives us a print of an etching, nobody would call him an artist, even if it cannot be denied that we have his industriousness to thank for a very beautiful object. We do not permit him to be called an artist because the features that constitute the etching's beauty were not first produced by his own technique as he was creating the print, but only came to be as a result of the particular procedure of the etcher or the creator of the drawing [from which the etching was made]. Moreover, a *causal* connection between the work's beauty and the technique of its creator is not sufficient. The creator must also have *anticipated* the beauty and must have executed his technique with the specific *intention* of producing it. After all, nobody will view as a work of art the foam on the mouth of the horse that a painter is alleged to have evoked so convincingly when he threw his sponge at the canvas in a fit of rage;[4] rather, it will be viewed as a work of chance. Indeed, we are not even disposed to recognize a

---

4. [The reference is to an anecdote about an ancient painter, either Apelles or Protogenes, who grew so frustrated, when trying to depict the foam on the horse's mouth, that he threw his sponge at his work, thereby getting exactly the effect that had eluded him.]

very beautiful object as an authentic work of art if it was created not with intent, but only as a result of its creator having, through regular practice, made the actions that brought it forth a matter of habit and second *nature*. This is why we draw a distinction between the *artificial* and the *natural* or what has only gradually *become nature* through art. The distinction, by the way, does not lead us to minimize the beauty and value of the latter. The inestimable benefits brought forth by industrious engagement with good writing consist in the fact that it enables us to act in a noble manner and avoid doing anything crude or low, both in everyday situations, where we do not deem it worth the energy to pay any particular mind to our behavior, and in moments where great excitement distracts us from thinking about how we perform our actions. This is what the poet meant by the words:

> . . . *didicisse fideliter artes*
> *Emollit mores, nec sinit esse feros.*[5]

3

According to this explication, it seems inherent to the concept of *art* that, when practicing art, we have to follow certain rules and set certain aims, which ensure that the end result has precisely one type of beauty and not any other. Although we are not always distinctly conscious of these rules, intensive contemplation makes it possible to trace them back to concepts articulated clearly and distinctly. This will indeed be the lofty task that a theory of art will have to undertake. A theory of art should tell us, with the greatest possible clarity, *how* beautiful works of art come into being. It should describe to the artist, on the one hand, how he already acts when producing artworks and, on the other, how he must act in the future to produce works with a greater degree of perfection.

---

5. [A careful study of the liberal arts / Refines manners and prevents them from being savage.—Ovid, *Ex Ponto* II.9 47–48.]

4

Against this, many claim that the fine arts *cannot* be taught at all. If they were right, then the concept that I have allocated to the theory of art would be contradictory. What *cannot* be taught cannot have a field of study dedicated to teaching it. But this is not how things are. Rather, it is only true that nobody to whom nature has not already granted a singular talent could be put in a position to create a competent artwork by being taught mere rules and written prescriptions. However, it in no way follows from this that artists, both beginning and advanced, cannot be given guidance on how they should proceed when practicing their art.

1. First, every work of fine art exerts many effects on us in addition to delighting us with its beauty. These effects should not be ignored. In some cases, they are perhaps the more important aspect of the work, so that its beauty only appears as something subordinate and should be treated as such. So then, should it be impossible to say anything that is worth the attention of the novice artist about these matters? Matters that he would all too certainly overlook in his moments of enthusiasm, if he had not already made himself familiar with them? Nothing about these various effects and their relation to beauty? Nothing about how such diverse ends must be simultaneously pursued in art and about how one end can be sacrificed for the benefit of another?

2. If a work of art is to be accessible to many recipients, then it must either endure in the external world or be renewed from time to time. This can happen only when the artist understands how to form some raw material provided to him by nature into an expression of the ideas that live inside him. And the more perfectly he succeeds in this, the more admiration we show his work. Nobody will say that, for this *technical aspect* of art, many skills and techniques that can only be obtained through lessons are not necessary.

3. Think of how much insight and experience an artist must possess just to generate the *internal* model that will guide him in his artistic shaping of the external world and to complete his internal model to such a degree that his work will never be anything more than a weak realization of it, one less ready to satisfy him than anyone else! And

think of how those insights and experiences must have been made so habitual that he can act in line with them without ever being distinctly conscious of them! As we know, something can only be beautiful if it is regular, so that, by observing some of its parts, we can discern neither all too easily nor all too laboriously the rules that guided its formation. If it is a product of *human* activity, then we are justified in expecting that it was produced for a rational purpose. We never find a work truly beautiful if we cannot at least obscurely grasp what purpose all of its parts and attributes might have. Now, is one to believe that the artist will meet all these demands if he has not reflected, often and intensely, on works of the same type as his own, and on the features that they must not lack? If he has not completed preliminary "*studies,*" painstaking studies? Do you believe that everything just comes to him from out of nowhere? That the Muses waste their inspiration on those who have worked not at all to receive their favor? It is certainly true that artists themselves are often unable to properly explain the thoughts that led them to a certain idea. However, nobody should deceive themselves into believing that more than just *isolated* serendipitous ideas come to the artist without further ado; nobody should flatter himself into thinking that he can successfully create a whole artwork composed of many parts if he has not gathered thoughts about his object over the course of many years. And everyone should acknowledge it as indisputable that, among a group of artists to whom nature has gifted equal talents, the one who is most immersed in the nature of the beautiful and the conditions of its emergence will be the one who will create the more perfect work of art.

4. All of this is proven by experience itself. Even the greatest genius—as every page of the *history of the fine arts* teaches us—even the most brilliant minds who did not have any lessons or direction on their art and who did not even have examples and preparatory work with which they could exercise and cultivate their judgment—such as so-called *natural poets* or *autodidacts*—never created anything entirely perfect in its kind. Instead, in their works we always encounter, alongside unsurpassable beauty, such crude deficiencies and mistakes as could have been avoided under other circumstances. Novice artists benefit from the study of even just *a few* examples and from producing a few very imperfect practice works. How else can this occur than by

their inferring a kind of theory from their observation of these examples, which they subsequently follow in their own work? Than by their ruminating on the impressions that the exemplary work made on them and discerning what is beautiful in it and what is not, what they should imitate and what they should take care to avoid? And if such an admittedly very imperfect theory is useful to them—a fact that we can perceive in how their work exhibits greater perfection when they adhere to it—then how are we to believe that there will be no utility in a theory of art that seeks to shine light on the ultimate reasons for our pleasure in the beautiful and then to deduce from them a series of prescriptions for artists? How could such a theory of art be anything other than a lodestar both for artists and for the critics who judge them, a lodestar that can serve as a reliable guide for their actions and as a stable foundation for their judgments?

5

There are scholars who deny that a theory of art has any real benefit, or could possibly ever have any real benefit. However, in recent times, there has been no lack of those with such exaggerated expectations about the scope and significance of this field of study that they have even gone so far as to make the erroneous claim that the theory of art or, more specifically, kalobiotics has an importance and scope that is the same as, if not greater than, *morality*. They assert that the theory of art ultimately extends to every human act executed with free will, because every such act is to be viewed as an object that is subject to the prescriptions of kalobiotics. In short, they claim that every such act is itself to be viewed as a work of art. After all, they ask, should we not be able to give every act a certain degree of beauty, if we focus on doing so? And should it not be demanded of us as a duty to strive for perfection as much as possible? There is some truth in this. We humans are indeed to be reprimanded. We rob ourselves of many joys of life when we too seldom think about how we could, with a little effort, make whatever we are doing much more beautiful and thus much more enjoyable, both for ourselves and others. I praised Wilhelm Bronn above for pointing out this shortcoming of ours and for offering multiple suggestions for how to ameliorate it. Yet it would be a tremendous exaggeration (of which, by the way, the respectable scholar just referenced is in no way guilty) to demand that we should take into serious consideration the laws of the beautiful when choosing how to perform all, or even close to all, of the acts that we perform of our own volition and can thus execute as we please. In short, it would be a tremendous exaggeration to demand that we turn each of these acts into a sort of *artwork*. Sometimes, the act would be so trivial and fleeting that we would look *ridiculous* were we to stop and contemplate how we might execute it in line with the rules of the beautiful. In other instances, the opposite would hold: the act would be so significant and there would be afforded us so little time for contemplation that we might even *sin* were we to stop and consider such an issue. Certainly, those who are familiar with the general laws of the beautiful and who have made a habit of following them will act accordingly, without thinking about it, even in such situations as these. Then we will be permitted to ascribe beauty to their acts. But the most beautiful thing about the act will always be its quality of being purposeful and morally good, so good in these respects that we can rest assured that the agent had no need for any guidance regarding how their actions are to be made beautiful. Therefore, guidance on the beautiful will only be warranted *when we are dealing with the production of an object that we can allow ourselves time to reflect on and that we seek to preserve and make communicable to others, such that it is reasonable to expect that many people will sooner or later observe it with pleasure and benefit, which will be augmented in proportion to the number of beautiful qualities that we have given it.*

This general proposition makes it possible to assess the scope of a theory of art or, above all, an aesthetic that does not want to exceed its limits. It makes it possible to assess which products of human activity the field of study is not only justified in giving directions about but also those about which it is obligated to give directions. The field of study need not comment, for instance, on how we should walk or stand, on how we should hold our hands, or on how we should do thousands of other things. This is not to say that there can be nothing beautiful or ugly in these things. But the field of study will just have to declare that some things that are purposeful in other respects can be beautiful and the opposite are ugly, all the while setting everything else aside as beyond its remit. The theory of fine art will be even less concerned with prescribing the ornamental movements we should make when leaping into the water, trying to save someone who has fallen in, or with prescribing the gestures and words that we should use to express the infinite pain that grips us when a loved one passes away. Neither here nor there should we be disposed even to consider the precepts of aesthetics. Are there not too many people already who, in their overly strict regard for what they call the laws of fine living, have lost all of their naturalness and so do not give us pleasure but repulse us instead?

6

So, if the relation between the *theory of art* and *aesthetics* is as close as we described it in §1, then it must be one of the most important tasks of the latter to give us an *overview* of all arts that deserve to be called *fine arts* and to properly determine the concept of each one. Scholars have indeed sought to do so in the past, and even *Umbreit*, who denies the need for a classification of the fine arts for aesthetics, does not dispense with such an overview.[6] However, I permit myself to offer my own thoughts on this matter, because previous attempts diverge so markedly from one another, particularly in respect to the criteria that inform their classifications.

Above all, I believe something that others have also recognized: one must distinguish between *simple* and *complex* arts. In the task that we are confronted with, it is not primarily a matter of not overlooking any of the arts that might be complex, but of not overlooking any of the simple arts.

When should we call an *art*—or, what ultimately amounts to the same thing, an *artwork*—*simple* and when *complex*? Everyone will certainly grant that we do the latter when the practice of an art must combine the activities of two or more other arts. However, I anticipate that many will smirk haughtily in disagreement when I remark that

---

6. August Ernst Umbreit, *Aesthetik* (Leipzig: Barth, 1838), 171.

this explication tells us practically nothing if we do not first determine what constitutes an *individual* art and what constitutes two or more arts and when I claim that it is not just a matter of our arbitrary choice as to whether we recognize something to be the product of a single art and another to be the product of two or more arts. Rather, we must decide according to a principle that I put as follows: *we may view as belonging to a single art only those practices whose parts cannot, for reason of their nature, be split up or distributed among multiple individuals for execution and, moreover, whose teaching requires a continuous course of study* [Anleitung], *as the one part cannot be understood or applied without the other.* But why do I expect that this claim will be met with haughty smirks of disagreement? I dare say that it is simply because it is much too obvious, too much in line with common sense, and because it presents itself much too straightforwardly to satisfy the taste *of our time.* Now, because I am accustomed not to let such considerations pressure me to abandon an opinion whose correctness I have verified through repeated examination, I will stick by what I have said until somebody shows me better. Thus, I assert that an art can only be called *simple* when it prescribes practices that are so internally related to one another that they can only be properly executed by a single person and that teaching them requires a continuous course of study, for otherwise it could not be properly understood or effectively applied. I call a work of art *complex* and the art of which it is an instance a *complex art* only when the production of the work of art requires practices that are, in general, carried out by different individuals or at least stand in such a loose relationship to one another that it is most practical to teach them separately. With this, I aim only to act in the spirit of those whom we have to thank for the invention of the various fine arts or the first theories of them. Because even if they did not come up with a *name* (which is actually not that important) for each and every art that I treat as a *simple* art according to the aforementioned explication and even if they omitted to immediately treat the theory of each art in its own treatise (something that, out of modesty and other considerations, we could manage without having, so long as the scope of such a theory was not yet very extensive), they did nevertheless determine what constitutes its own simple art by *dividing up* the arts. For instance, reciting a speech, *declamation,* is indisputably its own art, which has always been distinguished from the art of composing a speech. Even speeches composed with particular words have always been divided into two parts: the *thoughts* communicated in them and their *expression in language*. Separate lessons were given for the one (*de inventione*) and for the other (*de elocutione*), a practice that demonstrates that lessons were being given in two distinct arts, even if this was not explicitly stated. The same happened in treatises on *literary art*. The fact that even the most common people view the translation of a poem into another language not as a *new* poem but as the *same poem* enables us to clearly see that they regard the mere *collection of thoughts* articulated in the poem as a poem in and of itself and thus as a work of art. Indeed, it demonstrates that they see this collection of thoughts as such a valuable work of art that, when they view the work in the light of the creation of these thoughts, they consider the work performed by someone who translates the thoughts into another language hardly worth mentioning.

7

Accordingly, in my opinion, there are as many *simple arts* as there is *guidance* for particular artistic activities that can be beneficially separated from one another, each treated as a whole. Similarly, there are as many *complex arts* as there is guidance for particular artistic activities that can be beneficially *unified* with one another, revealing themselves in this unity to be a useful whole.

Now, we may certainly be permitted to hope that we will not overlook any of the more important arts, especially none of those known in our time and none of those that deserve to be called simple arts. Our investigation will involve going through all of the products that humans are capable of making through their free and intentional activity (obviously, never without more or less assistance from the external world that surrounds them, without which they could not for a moment survive), examining each one as indicated in §6. This will enable us to determine whether or not each product constitutes a work of art and whether it would be generally useful to introduce specific *guidance* for products of the same kind—or whether the guidance already exists. However, because we are not capable of studying every single one of the countless human products in existence but can only study them gathered together, it will be expedient to treat genera as *simpler* genera if there are, among their products, at least *some* that are simpler than the products of the other genera, adhering to an order that places these simpler genera before the others. For instance, the genus of *representations* contains, on the whole, simpler products of the human mind than does the genus of *propositions*, because every proposition is composed of representations. So we will place the genus of mere representations before that of propositions. The expectation is not that *all* arts that come under the purview of this genus—because their products belong to the genus of mere representations—will be simple arts. The expectation is rather that the simple arts whose products belong to the genus of mere representations—if, indeed, such arts exist—will reveal themselves to us more readily than if we were to try to discover them without using such a guide.

8

This perspective on the greater or lesser simplicity of an art can hardly be the *only* one that we need for an orderly overview of all the fine arts. We must undoubtedly acknowledge a few other factors that can be proven to have contributed to the emergence of the fine arts.

1. The *first* and most important of these is the *purpose* that we demand that the artist seek to attain in his work through certain actions or that the artist himself actually sought to attain in his work. On the whole, the work's purpose will require that the artist endow his work with a multitude of features, so that it may receive praise for its design. Many of these features will be determined in advance, while only some, perhaps only a few of them, will be left to the artist's free choice—and only such that they stand in harmony with the work's purpose, or at least do not contradict it. As there are many different purposes, each work must have attributes that are in line with its specific purpose. And it often takes special training to be able to recognize these purposes and, once one has recognized them, to make a work that actually attains them. Now, if the purposes are ones whose pursuit

cannot be considered only in and for themselves, but that we must wish to be very often pursued and attained for the good of humanity, then there will be no argument about whether guidance as to how to make the works in question can justifiably constitute its own *theory of art.* This has long been known, and most extant arts distinguish themselves from one another only in respect of the varying purposes that they seek to attain with the greatest possible beauty. However, I must express disapproval when some (as *Krug* has done)[7] take this difference between the arts as an occasion to separate them into two classes, one being *the absolutely beautiful* arts—that is, those that have no other purpose than that of *beauty* (the satisfaction of taste)—and the other being the *relatively beautiful*—that is, those that also fulfill other purposes. This is not correct. Rather, every rational human act— even more so every act that is executed with as much contemplation as the production of an artwork—must have been intended and executed with more purposes in mind than merely providing pleasure in beauty. This is made clear by the simple fact that this purpose alone, were it to be the same in every work of art, would not permit works of art to differ from one another. All absolute works of art would have to be the same as one another, there could be no rational basis to design the one like this and the other like that, and their variations would be irra- tional. That would constitute the first deficiency we would notice in a supposed work of art, and it would occasion our displeasure. Imagine, for instance, that Horace intended that we be able to perceive in even just one of his *Epistles* or *Odes* really no other purpose than that he wanted to offer us something beautiful: must we not then declare it to be a failed work of art?

9

2. While the different purposes to be achieved by an artwork offer one very important factor in the classification of many arts, the different

7. [Wilhelm Traugott Krug, *Versuch einer systematischen Enzyklopädie der schönen Künste* (Leipzig: Hempel, 1802).]

means that the artist uses to achieve these purposes represent a no less important factor in classifying many others.

I understand means to include not simply the objects that the artist uses as *tools* or *rules* in his work. I also understand with this concept the *component parts* or the *material* out of which he *composes* his work of art. Thus means will not only comprise the musical instrument that an artist uses to perform a piece of music but also the canvas and paints that an artist uses to produce a painting. These examples suffice to remind us just how significant an influence various means exert on an artist's practice, and they remind us that these various means require their own forms of guidance or theories of art.

10

3. Finally, consideration must be given to *limitations of human nature* and the *diversity* of *bodily and mental powers and dispositions*. While focusing on one thing and familiarizing ourselves with it through practice, we cannot at the same time engage in another activity. And not everybody has the same disposition and power for every type of free, rational action. Rather, one person will be successful primarily in one activity, while another will be successful primarily in another. For this reason, too, it is necessary to separate some arts and the guidance concerning them, so that everyone can select for themselves the one for which they have a natural aptitude.

11

With these preliminaries out of the way, we may now proceed without hindrance to address our task, beginning by answering the question: *What are the simplest products of free human activity that can be called works of art?*

Every work of art must be something real, but it does not have to be an object that exists in *external reality*. That is, it does not have to be an object that is perceptible by means of the *external senses*. After all, among the products that, taken for themselves, are nothing but *internal mental* processes, there are (as we saw in §7) some that general consensus regards as works of art, for which theories of art have already existed for centuries (such as Aristotle's *Poetics* and *Rhetoric*).[8]

But when they are reduced to their simple component parts, all mental phenomena (which I admittedly cannot prove here, but must presume to have been proven elsewhere) can be categorized as belonging to one or more of the following types.[9] They are either mere representations (which, for their part, can be pure concepts, pure intuitions, or mixed representations), or they are complete propositions (which must be true or false; inferences [*Schlüsse*] are only a particular type of proposition). We subsume both representations as well as propositions under the common name "thoughts" (among which we also count those representations and propositions that only obscurely appear to us and are generally referred to as feelings). I further distinguish between gratifying, unpleasant, and mixed sensations; wishes (desires and repulsions), which follow out of our sensations as an effect follows out of its cause; and, finally, resolutions of the will, which freely decide between what we wish to do and what we should do.

Now, there is no need to demonstrate that, although they might often possess much beauty, sensations, wishes, and resolutions of the will are not to be considered genuine works of fine art in the sense determined above. In other words, it is not to our purpose to develop an art or theory to tell us how we can give the highest degree of beauty to our sensations, wishes, and resolutions of the will.

For, at least as far as our sensations and wishes are concerned, everybody knows that they are not products of our free intentional action but that they appear in us without our doing anything; indeed, they often appear in us entirely against our will. And insofar as we can indirectly exert considerable influence on our sensations and wishes, whom do I really need to tell that this influence is so entirely

---

8. [Aristotle 1987 and Aristotle 2018.]

9. Many of the concepts in the following can be found in their respective places in my *Theory of Science* [Bolzano 2014(1837): esp. §§19, 25, 48, 72–73].

determined by the dictates of moral law that no room remains for the rules of the beautiful? When, for instance, would we be permitted to seek to evoke a desire in ourselves just because that desire is beautiful and not because it would make us happy and at the same time promote the welfare of others? More precisely, what other attribute would constitute the beauty of a desire but that it promoted the welfare of others?

As far as resolutions of the will are concerned, the term itself makes clear that they are totally free products of our mind. But it is all the more undeniable that they have no other beauty than that of their morality, which, I say, already contains the rationality, cleverness, and every other perfection that one might add to it to increase its beauty.

12

Thus it remains only to consider the few internal mental processes that I distinguished above with the concepts "representation" and "proposition" and then brought together under the heading "thoughts."

Accordingly, let us first inquire into whether there indeed exist arts consisting of mere representations—that is, into whether the mere production of a (it goes without saying, complex) representation could sometimes be called a work of art. Closer reflection will make it clear that not just some but all works of art that consist in an object in external reality could never have been produced by their creator through his free and intentional action if he had not first been able to develop a very detailed representation of the object in his mind. And although we would not claim that his entire art consists in the creation of an internal representation, its creation is certainly a great, and in some cases indeed the greatest, part of his entire art. As we know, the internal representation is already a work of art in itself. In creating it, the artist even follows many rules with more or less distinct consciousness, and, if he is rational, he would be happy to find these rules correctly laid out and demonstrated in a theory of art. Thus, for every distinct art or work of art of the external senses that we encounter below, we must assume that there is a corresponding art or work of art of the inner sense, of mere representation.[10] Indeed, for this reason, it will be sufficient for our current purposes simply to have recalled this point, and nobody will demand from us a list of every single one of these arts.

13

However, I do not think that there is any other type of artwork of mere representations, aside from that noted above, although I also do not think I could prove with the concepts laid out here that such an artwork would be impossible. But even that type of artwork that would most appear to consist of mere representations, namely, the poem, seems upon closer inspection to consist in propositions. Even if the poet does not intend that we view them as truths and even if we entirely set aside whether they are true, he offers them to us so that we might give space in our minds to the feelings, sensations, wishes, and resolutions of the will that their contemplation might occasion in us. If this concept of poetry is correct (it will be elucidated in a later essay),[11] then the *poem* would be the first type of artwork that consists of complete propositions.

> The revered goddess from whom every sweet gift stems,
> Bestows upon the untrue the charms of the true,
> Whose splendor dazzles the world.
> —Pindar, *Ol.[ympian]* 1[12]

---

10. I was happy to learn that Dr. Hebenstreit shares this opinion in his *Encyklopädie der Ästhetik* (in the articles on music, partiture, etc.) [Wilhelm Hebenstreit, *Wissenschaftlich-literarische Encyklopädie der Aesthetik* (Wien: Gerold, 1843)].

11. [The later essay was not written. Here Bolzano retracts his claim in Bolzano 2014(1837): §284 that poems consist in representations, not propositions.]

12. [Bolzano quotes the German translation by Johannes Minckwitz, *Gedichte* (Leipzig: Kummer, 1847), 45. That version is translated here. A recent translation directly from the Greek is: "Grace, who fashions all gentle things for men, / Confers esteem and often contrives to make believable the unbelievable"—Pindar, *Odes*, trans. Diane Arnson Svarlien (1990) < http://www.perseus.tufts.edu/hopper/text?doc=urn :cts:greekLit:tlg0033.tlg001.perseus-eng1:1>.]

14

If there are collections of propositions that deserve our full attention, even without our inquiring into whether what is asserted in them is true or false (and even if we have determined that it is the latter), then it is obvious that collections of propositions that state truths are, under certain circumstances, even more deserving of our attention. How much, how infinitely much, can we humans gain through knowledge of important truths, since all our values and all our happiness are rooted in our opinions and convictions! Blessed be humanity when the time comes when every useful truth can be found in a fine treatise and everything everywhere is presented in the most easily comprehended fashion and proven in the most convincing manner, and when, moreover, every available means is employed to outfit all of it with so much charm and beauty that all who have the necessary talent feel themselves most powerfully attracted and gripped when they read these books! But a condition must be met to reach this goal and, once attained—due to the constant progress of human knowledge, which makes possible and requires a constant progress in these treatises—to ensure that it does not escape us again. That is, we must first take care that, if it does not already exist, guidance is very soon written about how to compose all of these books, each of which must be, in its own way, a true work of art. Indeed, the need for such guidance has already been recognized, and such theories of art have long existed; it is desirable only that they achieve even greater perfection. This last point can be facilitated, at least in part, by determining more precisely than in the past just how many of these theories of art there should be and which task each of them should address.

15

The truths that humanity needs to know are divided into two types: purely conceptual truths and truths of experience (propositions composed of mixed representations). Not everyone who is able to deal proficiently with the one has the disposition to learn how to deal with the other. Even in the field of empirical truths, it makes a difference whether we just have to describe the objects that lie before the senses or narrate events that occur in succession, or whether we have to deduce conclusions from immediately certain facts—or facts that may be considered certain—by drawing on some purely conceptual truths. One thing is sure, the occupations of some require them to work just with one or the other, and it is their obligation to learn how to use it with the greatest possible perfection. Finally, only some people have the ability—and only some are required in their circumstances—to influence the sensations and desires of others and induce them to make morally good decisions. Thus, we have reason to distinguish between at least five more arts of mere thought (of connecting propositions) in addition to poetry:

1. beautiful conceptual art, by which I mean the art involved in connecting thoughts in such a way that they provide insights into pure conceptual truths (such as philosophy and mathematics), such that they are, at the same time, through their beauty, genuine works of art;

2. descriptive art or the art of beautiful descriptions;

3. narrative art or the art of beautiful narratives;

4. the art of demonstrating empirical truths;

5. the art of evoking certain sensations, wishes, or resolutions of the will through the mere exposition of certain truths.

16

What I have assumed at several points so far is also generally acknowledged to be true: the arts of mere thought interact with each other in many respects. For instance, how often does an orator find it necessary, in a single speech, to expound on pure conceptual truths at one point, then call on experience, then lay out facts, then give proofs, and then finally stir his listeners' sentiments, and so forth? In my opinion, what has long been neglected is the use of literary art in all works intended for *teaching*.[13] The drier the principles of some sciences, such as mathematics, the more important it is to use literary art in all works intended for teaching. The more that certain principles—such as those of morality and religion—are intended not just to be grasped by the understanding but to be made so familiar that we automatically think of them in any situation where we are supposed to be guided by them, the greater the need to teach them in a way that is not completely detached from everything except their essential logical connections. In short, the greater the need not to teach them in a totally abstract way. On the contrary, they must be taught so as to engage as many sensory representations as possible, representations whose sensory nature appeals to everyone. Hence, they must be taught in the most diverse guises and forms. Although they can largely be taken from the real world (from history, etc.), they are most appealing, not just to young people but to people of all ages, when they come in the form of the vivid presentations of poetry, narrative, oratory, and the like.

17

The arts of mere thought that we have discussed up to this point are all afflicted with a grave imperfection. Since their products have no external existence, they are not artworks of the sort that are apprehended in a way that can be immediately communicated to others and provide them with knowledge and pleasure. Humans (with the exception of some uncommon cases, such as those born deaf, etc.) are so accustomed to using a language, specifically a sonic language, that they cannot represent their own thoughts to themselves in a clear manner without first articulating them in the vocabulary of their language and communicating them to others. For this reason, not even the creator of a beautiful collection of concepts can confidently and easily view his own creation anew—as often as he might wish to do in order to take pleasure in it or further perfect it—unless he has thought up and determined upon the word through which each thought is to

---

13. [These remarks are developed in detail in Bolzano 2014(1837): book 5.]

be expressed. The task of thinking up words that suit our thoughts is not easy, even when we do not devise new words ourselves but simply want to select them from an already existing vocabulary. There is much to consider here. There are many ways to express one and the same thought in the same language, and not all should be seen as equivalent to the others. The distinctive sounds of one expression can cause it to affect us differently than another expression. The associations that usage has attached to one expression can cause it to affect us differently than another expression that evokes other associations, and the like. Combining multiple words and series of words will establish relations between them that also demand attention. Words can clash with other words because of their sound, the length of their syllables, and other factors, or the opposite can occur and their unity can produce a whole with its own particular charms. All of this takes place and can even be felt (although perhaps only to a small degree) when we do not audibly speak the collection of words that express our collection of thoughts but only imagine them to ourselves in silence. Understandably, if we have a natural talent for this, if we receive good lessons, and if we spare no effort or hard work, then a collection of words can be assembled that has its own unique beauty and that deserves to be called a unique work of art. But insofar as words and the interconnections that compose a collection of words are not either spoken or represented in written signs, the collection will have just as little external existence as the mere collection of thoughts to which it gives expression. It remains a mere entity of thought, even if it is a quite different entity of thought from the one to which it gives linguistic expression. If it is sufficiently beautiful to be called a work of art at all, then a merely thought collection of words belongs to those works of art that we called works of mere representation in §12. By contrast, we now turn to actual collections of words that belong among the artworks of external reality.

18

Following on the arts of mere thought discussed up to this point, we now turn to those arts to which it is essential that their products have a sensory existence in the external world. We might thus call them *arts of the external senses*. Now, all objects that have a sensory existence belong to one of two genera.

We consider them either as *enduring*, by which we understand only those that, at least during the time that we view them, do not undergo any noticeable changes that alter their essence. Or we consider them as mere changes, as appearances in the strict sense, as things that, during the time we observe them, undergo changes that we consider to be essential to what they are. Clearly, there are artworks of both types, as the examples of a statue and a piece of music demonstrate. Thus, we will classify the arts [of external sense] in two categories: the *enduring* artworks and the *temporary* artworks.

19

At the same time, we must combine this classification with a second one determined by the nature of the senses with which we perceive a work of art. In my first essay [§16.2], I already touched on why the perceptions of the so-called lower senses are hardly suited to evoke that singular feeling in us that we call pleasure in the beautiful. Among the arts that produce objects that satisfy the needs of these lower senses or provide for pleasure, we will, insofar as they do not accomplish anything else, not find any genuinely fine arts. And I say this without wanting to neglect too much the value of these arts or to forget that one of them, culinary art, will deserve great respect once it recognizes and seeks to fulfill its true purpose—that is, when it tasks itself with teaching people not only how to prepare tasty foods but also foods that promote health, and in such a way that the act of cooking destroys the fewest nutrients possible.[14]

Consequently, among the arts of the external senses, only those are genuinely to be called fine arts that work either for the *eye* or the *ear*. Now, whether we begin our inquiry with the one or the other does not

---

14. [Bolzano elsewhere identifies famine and malnourishment amongst the most severe problems of his era (2007: 322–23).]

make much difference. Nonetheless, it seems more apt to begin with the sonic arts and then to proceed to the visual arts. Although the sense of sight might in some ways appear to us more important and even nobler than that of hearing, there are some considerations that make the sense of hearing much more conducive for launching our inquiry, an inquiry that seeks an organized overview of the fine arts and that also shows how they come into being one after the other. First, there is a closer connection between mere thought and productions for the ear—among which we must certainly place audible language at the very top—than there is between mere thought and productions for the eye. Second, song and music certainly existed much earlier than drawings, paintings, and sculptures. Finally, artworks of thought can be made perceptible to the ear either immediately or mediated by words—which are productions for the ear—whereas they can be made perceptible to the eye only through an intermediary (namely, writing).[15]

20

Since we first want to focus exclusively on the arts for the *ear,* which are also called *sonic* arts, it seems necessary for me to begin with a reminder that we can only really consider works of sonic art that are not also at the same time works of another type of art, such as works of the arts of thought discussed above. In particular, we may not consider any works of art in which the sounds played for our ears are also words that signify a coherent collection of thoughts, which would constitute a work of art in itself. Nor may we consider works of sonic art in which the artist's intentionally chosen sounds or sonic relations—even if they are not words—evoke in us a collection of thoughts that, although they might not count as anything higher, can at least be counted as poetic [*dichterischen*] thoughts. In this case, too, the work of art would have to be treated as complex. Finally, if we want to judge the value of the sonic artwork per se, we may not consider anything that affects our

---

15. [Bolzano later walks back the claim that artworks of thought cannot be made immediately visually perceptible (§34.1).]

sense of sight during its performance, such as the artist's beautiful, noble figure, his movements, or his posture.

21

The *first* question that arises here is whether products for the sense of hearing that qualify as works of art belong to the class of artworks that we defined in §18 as enduring works. Clearly, such a product could only consist of a collection of sounds that, for the entire time we are listening, continue with the same volume, in the same pitch, in the same purity, and harmonize perfectly. But as much as I might admit that even a single tone (see the first essay, §19.1), even more so a collection of multiple tones in harmony, could be listened to with pleasure, and even with pleasure of the kind that we sense in contemplating the beautiful, I think that this pleasure would remain at a low intensity. Indeed, the persistent monotony of a series of sounds that we view not as the work of happenstance but as the intentional production of an artist would not strike us as purposeful, so that we would not be inclined to recognize it as a genuine, successful work of art. After all, when listening to such a composition, must we not arrive at the conclusion that, with no more exertion than is needed to produce perpetually constant tones, varying them in an expedient way would have furnished incomparably greater enjoyment? And that, because of this, a collection of perpetually constant tones, viewed as a work of art, has something inappropriate about it that flies in the face of beauty?

Hence we will hardly be reproached when we demand that a product that is supposed to be a sonic work of art should comprise a whole composition of sounds that change in various ways when played for the ear of the recipient.

Here we will further distinguish between two types of sonic artworks, depending on their degree of completion [*Vollendung*]:

1. those in which the artist sought to cultivate as much beauty as possible without following, or binding himself to, rules that concern both duration and tonal pitch and that he intended the listener to notice and see as responsible for the beauty of the whole;

2. those that do cultivate this type of beauty [i.e., are products of following rules about duration and pitch].

Sonic works of art of the first type could be called *unconstrained*; those of the second type, *constrained*. If it is only the *duration* of the sounds used that is constrained by a rule that can be noticed by the listener, thereby augmenting the pleasure that they experience when perceiving the whole, then one can say that the artwork has rhythm. If it is only the pitch of the tones used that is constrained by such rules, then one can say that the artwork has *melody* or is melodic. And if both are true, then one can say that the work of art is *music* or a piece of music.

22

Second, we should consider the greater or lesser complexity of a sonic whole. The simplest type of sonic artwork is one in which the listener always hears only a single sound at any given point in time and the multiple sounds that must compose the sonic artwork, according to §21, follow upon one another successively. Such a sonic artwork can be called a *work for one voice*. Everybody knows that these artworks require their own art and their own form of guidance, because, in countless cases, one need and should do no more than make use of a single voice. Likewise, most people have to start off by learning this simple art before they are capable of performing or composing more complex pieces. We will therefore call the art a *simple sonic art*.

A complex artwork comes into being when multiple sounds (distinguishable to the listener) can be heard not only in succession but also simultaneously. I call this a *work for multiple voices* and remind the reader that it can, depending on the circumstances, be either unconstrained or constrained and, if constrained, can have a rhythm and can even constitute music.

Nobody will deny that in works where consonance occurs in one moment and dissonance in the next (and where certain tones can be entirely cancelled out through interference), special, often very complicated laws are applied and require their own form of guidance.

23

Third, if we consider the *means* that one employs to create the sounds involved in bringing forth a sonic artwork, we can distinguish primarily between *vocal* and *instrumental* works. The former are sonic artworks all of whose sounds are produced by the human voice. However, it is not necessary that these sounds articulate comprehensible words whose meaning the listener has to take into account. Only when there are no such words, as in so-called solfeggio, can the sonic artwork be considered a simple work of art. If there are comprehensible, connected words intended to absorb our attention in their own right, then it is a complex artwork of the sort that we will discuss shortly. Now, one might dispute whether it is not in itself inappropriate when a sonic work of art performed by a human voice is only composed of incomprehensible sounds, because a human mouth is capable of something much nobler. Nevertheless, it is indisputable that mere solfeggio has been found to be useful for teaching and that there are thousands of compositions by great composers that we find enchanting without text, or with a text that we cannot understand.

When they have a rhythm and melody, these vocal works of sonic art can often be called songs and may be contrasted with instrumental works of sonic art. Instrumental works are all those works in which, alongside or without the human voice, all kinds of other tools (musical instruments) are used more or less freely and intentionally (i.e., *playing* them), in order to call forth the most multifarious sounds.

We can now turn to assessing which different arts or different kinds of guidance are needed to use these various means for producing a sonic work of art. Such an assessment requires, above all, that we distinguish between two scenarios: scenarios in which the sonic artwork is created immediately, on the spot, and those in which it has already been created. In the latter case, the already created work is given to the performer with as great a degree of precision as is possible in a medium of signs that have been invented for the purpose (notes, etc.).

Nobody has ever doubted the need for special guidance in the first case, when the composer and performer are the same person, at least as concerns composition. In other words, nobody has ever doubted the necessity of an art of creating musical artworks.

In the second case, however, the question is how much or how little room there is for the free, intentional activity of the performer in their execution of the piece. And also whether the rules before him (the partiture) and the instrument that he is to play (in the case of instrumental music) are such that he can perform some things as he pleases and can even, through his knowledge of certain laws of the beautiful, augment the beauty of the sonic artwork that he is performing. Unless both of these conditions are satisfied, the technical proficiency that he needs to play his instrument might be very great and might only be learned through guidance and practice, yet his performance is not really a work of fine art, and the theory needed to perform it is not a genuine theory of art.

As far as the human voice in particular is concerned, our gracious creator gave healthy humans very broad latitude in choosing how they use it. Indeed, the degree of this latitude is such that the composer cannot entirely determine through mere written signs and indications how we perform his work, not even if it is a complete composition consisting of many sounds. Thus, the performer's own taste must play a role here. For this reason, guidance, a theory of art, is indispensable not only for the creation but also for the performance of already created and written works of vocal music.

24

Finally, if we direct our attention toward the *effect* intended by the creator of sonic works of art, we may primarily find the following types of works to be important:

1. sonic works of art that are supposed to evoke feelings of the *sublime* in us—for instance, admiration of God's omnipotence, wisdom, goodness, and the like;

2. sonic works of art that produce gentle *emotions*—for instance, those that incline us to reconcile with our enemies, to feel sympathy, to do good;

3. sonic works of art that are intended to *cheer us up* and make us happy about our lives.

Because experience teaches that one and the same artist rarely has the ability to achieve, just through the power of sounds, such divergent purposes with equal mastery, separate guidance is required for each of these types of sonic artwork. Incidentally, it is especially apparent here how the most important of the aforementioned purposes can only be achieved with a high degree of perfection when the human voice can be heard in sonic works not just in *comprehensible* sounds but in *words* with a meaning that commands attention in and of itself.

In this case, we are dealing with a work of art that deserves praise for its beauty not just because of its sounds as such, but also because of the thoughts that it evokes in us through its words. It is a work of art produced by unifying two arts, sonic art and an art of mere thought.

25

Let us now consider those complex works of art that can be created when a sonic art is unified with an art of mere thought, such that the one supports the effect of the other.

Closer observation shows that there are two distinct ways in which sonic art can be combined with an art of mere thought for the purpose of bringing forth an artwork.

I call the first the *direct* connection. It takes place when the sounds that enter our ears are selected in such a way that—although they may not contain a single comprehensible word, not to speak of cohesive sentences—they evoke certain series of thoughts in us that were intended by the artist and can be viewed as a kind of artwork of thought. That this is possible will be disputed by nobody who recalls how a single chord—and even more, a few successive tones—can occasion a sometimes solemn, sometimes joyful series of thoughts in one's imagination. On one hand, it may be true that much here depends on the listener's level of preparation and that various past experiences and other circumstances can cause some unique effects never foreseen by the artist. On the other, it is also true that there are certain laws rooted in human nature and in the general circumstances in which we grow up that allow us to expect, with a high degree of certainty, that certain sounds and sonic relations will occasion this or that feeling or series of thoughts in us. For instance, the laws in question allow us to anticipate that, when we hear the first tones of a melody that is customary in funeral processions, we will think of a funeral, and that we will think of conflict and confusion when the music seems to be off rhythm. Now, I gladly admit that these series of thoughts, which the artist intentionally prompts and guides in this or that direction, only rarely represent a very perfect artwork of thought. Nevertheless, works like this can be good enough to evoke quite appropriate sensations, wishes, and resolutions of the will in us, and they can realize the effect that the artist intends his sonic work to have. As far as their content is concerned, we will most often have to categorize them as fiction [*Dichtungen*], because they will be composed of a series of thoughts or propositions that we in no way consider to be true propositions but rather to be propositions that can occasion in us sensations, wishes, and resolutions of the will that we view as purposeful. If we have sufficient capacity to think—if we command a rich supply of important insights from all areas of human knowledge, over moral and religious truths, truths from history, natural science, and so forth—if we have all that, then it can happen that the representations immediately occasioned in us by the sensory artist's sounds will, through the sounds' associations with so many other representations, produce in us a collection of thoughts whose inventiveness is only a secondary matter and only serves to give form. Admittedly, we will not recognize such a collection of thoughts as a perfected work of art upon a given subject, but we will see it as a good draft for an artistic achievement that might belong to philosophy, world history, ethics, or some other field of study. In short, this is the first, direct mode in which musical art can be joined with an art of thought. In this mode, the artwork of thought is not actually produced by the artist, or at least not by him alone and not without the collaboration of the listener, but it must nevertheless be considered a work of his insofar as he is the one who occasions—and intentionally occasioned—these thoughts in us, giving them a specific direction. If we do indeed derive greater benefit from his work than he himself presumed would be the case, if it leads us to insights or beneficial resolutions of the will that he had never hoped to cause, if it affects the value and utility of his work, must he not be credited for all this, provided that his intention was good? We may indisputably call the sonic work of art that he produced a complex work of art, a work that unites sonic art and the art of thought that supports it.

The second, *indirect*, way in which sonic arts can be combined with arts of thought to produce a single work of art is well known. It is the complex art in which we first translate the artwork of mere thought into an artwork of the word and then have these words audibly performed in such a way that the beauty of the performance justifies acknowledging it, more or less, as a work of art in its own right, a work which will be recognized as a sonic work of art.

26

Were one to ask when we are justified in calling an artwork a *complex* one of the first type [where there is a direct connection], then we would draw the following answer from what has been said so far: only when it is shown that the artist selected and arranged sounds and their relations with the precise intention of evoking thoughts in the listener's mind that can be considered as a kind of artwork, or at least as a kind of *inventiveness*. And if one were to ask if there are many different artworks of this type, then I believe I would have to respond that the grand masters of sonic art seldom or never would be satisfied with an artwork that did not accomplish this. All great musical compositions contain more or less inventive elements, and you will discern traces of inventiveness even in the simplest melody that such a master deemed worthy of putting his name to. Accordingly, almost all artworks listed in §§22–25, which we considered only as simple musical works of art, remain simple only if they are rudimentary. As long as they are created by a competent master, they will raise the level of inventiveness—we need not list their names once again. And it is obvious that it will be necessary to have guidance for the production of these artworks in their perfect form, since guidance was already indispensable for them at a lower level.

27

Let us now turn to the second [indirect] mode of combining the arts of thought with sonic art. I take back nothing of what I said in §5 about how it would be inappropriate for aesthetics to meddle directly in how we should speak in everyday life. Nevertheless, in all cases in which we want to put an artwork of thought into words for the purpose of communicating it to others, I do demand that the beautiful thought be articulated in beautiful words, or, as the saying goes, that golden apples be presented in silver bowls. Thus, a collection of thoughts, so long as it is not just thought, but is also actually spoken out loud in accordance with its true purpose, must appear as an artwork. And it must appear as an artwork that is not only beautiful because of its content but because of the way it affects our sense of hearing; in short, it must appear as an artwork for the *ear*. This does not mean, however, that every work of this type must be written in verses and rhymes, or that one must *sing* it when performing it, and so forth. It would be highly inappropriate and in poor taste for a philosophical essay or a *speech* to be presented to our mind not according to its *conceptual content* but only according to its expression. Yet we can find certain aspects of beauty in the external form of intellectual products. It should not be misleading and should not call up distracting associations. A certain balance between thoughts and their expression should reign, and what is most important in thought should be emphasized in expression, and so forth. A theory that provides lessons for all of this is anything but superfluous. And separating it from guidance for the creation of mere thoughts will be very useful, because not everyone who has the skill to produce a beautiful collection of thoughts has the skill to clothe them in dignified words, and not everyone who has the latter skill is able to recite the words, at least not when serious singing is necessary.

I will allow myself to call artworks that emerge out of the appropriate joining of an art of mere thought (§15) with one or more sonic arts: artworks *of the word, of audible language,* or (because others have called it this before me) oratorial works of art or works of *oratory*. I distinguish between various types according to two different criteria:

1. I distinguish the following types of sonic works of art according to the quality of the *collection of thoughts* that give rise to an artwork upon being transferred into an appropriate audible language:

   a. the poem that is composed in words and recited,

   b. collections of pure conceptual truths, as discussed above,

   c. descriptions, as discussed above,

   d. narrations, or

   e. empirical proofs, and finally

   f. speeches in the strict sense, which aim to evoke certain sensations, wishes, and resolutions of the will by presenting certain truths.

2. I distinguish the following types of sonic artworks according to the quality of their *linguistic expression* and of the other sonic arts that support them:

   a. unconstrained recitations that fit well, for instance, with the artworks in points (b), (c), and (f) above;

   b. recitations that are constrained only with respect to a meter, and are called verses—for instance, epigrams;

   c. recitations that are constrained only with respect to melody, such as the style of singing the Gospel, Epistles, and the like that is customary in some branches of the Catholic church;

   d. recitations that are constrained with respect to both meter and melody, called singing in the strict sense, or songs;

   e. finally, singing with instrumental music.

Everybody who has read the preceding material will see how many different simple arts must work together in order for one of the kinds of artworks listed here to come into being.

28

Following the intention staked out in §19, we will now proceed to consider those arts whose products are perceived by our *sense of sight*.

We can call them *visual* arts. To begin with, there is no doubt that there must be at least two kinds of visual artworks: those that represent something *enduring* (something that does not noticeably change, at least not before our eyes), and those that *change* before our eyes. A second way of classifying the optical arts is given by the fact that our eyes, as is well known, can distinguish not only *colors* but also forms or *shapes*. Out of these considerations alone we can identify three very different types of optical artworks. The artist can

1. apply only one or more *colors* in such a way that a mere composition of colors itself evokes a feeling of the beautiful in us, even if we abstract from how they border one another [i.e., to make shapes]. Or the artist can work in such a way that our field of vision is at any given moment so absorbed by a single color that we have a sensation of infinite color, and we only focus on the impression that their succession evokes. Or the artist can

2. allow multiple colors to enter our field of vision at the same time but select them in such a way that we are practically indifferent to them as colors in themselves, and they only serve to bound each other in such a way that they create *shapes* that we perceive with pleasure. Upon reflection, everyone will admit that shapes could not be perceived by our eye without us seeing some color (and all light has color)—indeed, without our seeing two or more colors at the same time. After all, only those lines in which we perceive two distinct colors bordering on one another have a shape, and the colors give shape both to the surface enclosed by them and to the surface surrounding them. The intention of the artist can be that we sometimes focus on and find beautiful the line that separates the colors, sometimes the surface that is enclosed by them, and sometimes the surface that surrounds them. Finally, the artist can

3. combine *both* of these approaches and expect us to praise the beauty of both the shapes that draw our attention and also in the colors chosen to present them.

Closer inspection is needed to determine if and how the production of multifarious visual artworks is possible when we view these three types in combination with the criteria of *endurance* or *temporariness and alteration* discussed in §18, and the other variations that can result.

29

After everything that has been said up to now, one will readily admit that the appearance of a color that does not form a shape, that absorbs the viewer's entire field of vision,[16] and that is thus just one single color lacks all variety and so, for precisely this reason, can hardly be called a beautiful work in the genuine sense, much less an authentic work of art. Yet, in my opinion, it is not impossible to count as an artwork a series of colors that succeed one another at particular intervals, where each absorbs our entire field of vision for a period of time. This mere play of colors without shapes amounts to an artwork that may at best be called a chromatic work of art.

The first experiment of this sort, *L. B. Castel's* so-called color clavier, might have been a failure, and the suggestions for improvement made by *Kruger* and others might have been no more satisfying.[17] But who would conclude from this that every future attempt is destined to fail? It is certain that colors, like sounds, can fascinate us, albeit to a lesser degree. Furthermore, the close similarity between how colors and sounds are produced, perceived, judged, and distinguished is proven. It is also proven that the relationship that different colors have to one another is similar to the relationship that different sounds

---

16. Strictly speaking, the viewer would also assume they were looking at a shape—in particular, a sphere—only because the uniformity of the light shining toward him from every direction does not provide any grounds for surmising that some physical objects that the light makes visible are closer or farther away from him than any others. That the sky at its zenith appears closer than it does on the horizon is attributable to the fact that its color is significantly paler on the horizon than it is toward the zenith.

17. [In 1725, the French mathematician Louis Bertrand Castel announced his idea for an "ocular harpsichord." He built a rudimentary prototype in 1734 but never succeeded in realizing his vision. Johann Gottlob Krüger, a German professor of medicine, published plans for a more sophisticated device in 1743. See Franssen 1991.]

have to one another. Like our ear, our eye becomes bored by persistent monotony and, after viewing certain colors, wants to see some other colors, and so forth. So, then, why should colors not deserve to be seen as truly beautiful artworks, in the same way as sounds do, when they appear to us abstracted from the shapes that they can enable the eye to perceive—when they appear to have no limit at all—so long as they succeed one another in a fitting order and at fitting intervals? It cannot be denied that the power of sounds is much stronger than the power of colors, as I have repeatedly admitted. The power of sounds probably does not derive only from the fact that, as vibrations of a much cruder medium, they affect our nerves much more strongly (when we hear certain sounds, our chest and diaphragm perceptibly quaver, and inanimate objects around us resonate with the sound, sometimes even being shattered by strong sounds). For humans, the power of sounds likely derives above all from the fact that almost all of our stronger sensations are expressed through particular sounds and sonic relations (natural tones). Music consequently evokes the same kind of sensations in our mind, so long as it presents our ear with just a few tones sufficiently similar to these natural tones. However, this omnipotence of sounds is not the source of the pure beauty of music in the strict sense (see §17 of the first essay). Thus, while the power of colors might be significantly weaker than that of sounds, there could still be alternations of color that might bespeak the highest degree of beauty. To prevent us from an all too disparaging opinion of the power of colors, even in their state as mere colors, I will allow myself simply to remind the reader of the intensity with which certain colors can both attract and repulse not just children, but also creatures lower than we humans. Might not this magical influence, whatever its source, endure in us to a lesser degree, even after we have come of age and believe ourselves to have shed all childish inclinations through the training of our mental powers? And so I believe that one should not dismiss the possibility that a kind of *visual music* might yet be created. Imagine a hollow globe fashioned of colored glass that is illuminated from without as evenly as possible, while our eye is placed before an opening no narrower than would be needed to restrict the field of vision from seeing beyond the interior of the glass globe. This would certainly not be impossible to create. The sight we would behold would be as if the entire globe were evenly covered with one and the same color. Now imagine that one had multiple such globes in many different colors and a gadget were devised with which one could freely bring the globes into our field of vision in a fitting order and duration. And imagine that the gadget made it possible to prevent errant light from entering our field of vision as the globes changed, so that only a harmonious color would arise during these transitions. If one could develop such a setup, one could create a spectacle by combining a fitting choice of colors with a fitting choice of durations for each color and for the transitions between colors. If somebody accomplished all this, then I would hope, not without some confidence, that the spectacle would win its spectators' praise of its beauty. However, only then will it be the right time to decide whether a dedicated theory of this art, of visual music, deserves to be drafted.

30

Nobody who knows what *drawing* is can dispute that, among the visual arts, some are indifferent to color and only use it for the purpose of showing us *shapes*, *enduring* shapes at that (in the sense discussed above). After all, what we demand of a pure *drawing* is indeed that it represent forms and shapes that please us, regardless of the colors used to represent them. Moreover, what is significant is *how* the artist produces the shapes that we see. There is a key difference between two cases. In one, the shapes that the artist wants us to imagine as we contemplate his work are produced by *bodies that really bear these shapes*. In the other, the artist applies certain colors to a surface such that, when we view the surface from the proper perspective, our eye registers shapes in the light rays: the rays are arranged so that they come from the same directions as they would were a body of the intended shape actually in front of us. In addition to perceiving the intensity of the color of light, the eye can immediately perceive only its direction, but not the distance of its source. We can only infer distance probabilistically, by working with *instructions* that the *sense of sight* gives us. In particular, we infer the distance of the source based on the greater or lesser intensity of the light, as well as the apparent size of its angle of view

[*Gesichtswinkel*] in relation to that of an object that is already known to us.[18] Therefore, when viewing a colored surface, we might see rays of light that primarily originate from the area where two colors border on one another [creating an outline] and that meet our eye at an angle that is exactly the same as that of a body that we have seen frequently before from the same perspective. The well-known law of association, whereby certain representations are called up by other, similar representations, makes it no surprise that when this occurs it generates in us the *representation* of such a body, if not the belief that such a body is actually there before us. The representation is brought to mind not only when the colors are those that the body in question normally has, but also when they are completely different. What matters is only that the rays are so arranged that their direction outlines a shape similar to the body's shape.[19] Now, if the representation is such that it does not seem inconceivable that someone might have intentionally sought to evoke it in us, then we immediately task ourselves with trying to figure out the artist's aim through closer observation of all parts of the work before us. And if we succeed in this and determine that all parts of the work have been purposefully arranged, then we do not hesitate to declare it a work of art.

We can call the first of the two types of cases discussed here—that in which the artwork consists of bodies that themselves have the shape that we are supposed to perceive—a *plastic work*, and the art that delineates all the rules of producing such artworks, *sculpture*. The plastic artworks include, in addition to busts and statues, temples, palaces, and even living people, as well as mere letters.

---

18. [A *Gesichtswinkel* is a face angle, which is the angle subtended by two sides of a polyhedron. What Bolzano seems to be describing is a solid angle, or *Raumwinkel* in German. A solid angle is that subtended by the outline of a solid from a viewpoint.]

19. On this line of reasoning, the mere ordering of indifferent colors can evoke a *representation* of a certain shape in us only if we have often seen a similarly shaped body in the past. Anyone who still doubts that this is really so can easily convince themselves of its truth by experiments with themselves and with others. When viewing drawings that depict a shape that is totally unknown to us and that we have never seen before, we will know neither which parts are supposed to be imagined to be in the foreground and which in the background nor how or with which shape we should outline the represented thing.

We can call the second type *graphic* art, or *drawing*. But it must also include engravings, silhouettes, monochrome prints, and the like.

At the same time, it is worth noting that there are works that only *partially* take on the shapes that they represent, namely, *reliefs*, such as those found in cameos, coins, and the like. Among both *plastic* and *graphic* artworks, there is a great diversity in the objects that they represent, the means that they deploy, and the purposes that they intend to realize. It follows that there must be a great and ever-growing body of guidance for how to practice these arts, as well as theories about them. However, we do not need to list them. After all that has been said up to this point, everybody will be able to judge for themselves which of this guidance we can justifiably say constitutes its own theory of art.

31

Although we said that the different colors used in *artworks of mere shape* only serve the purpose of making certain *shapes* perceptible by mutually bounding one another, we in no way mean to imply that the artist can just randomly choose which colors to use. Anything that is not already determined by other factors should not be arranged by the artist haphazardly, but should be crafted in accordance with the laws of the beautiful or with other rules that the spectator can reconstruct when viewing the work. After all, the premier source of beauty in all human creations consists in the suitability of all their parts and the general ease in which this suitability can be grasped. For instance, no artist (unless he lives in a Moorish country) would paint the statue of a Medici Venus black, but would instead choose white, silver, or gold. But no matter what reasoning the artist might devote to selecting colors needed for a morphological work of art, none of it can augment the value of the shapes themselves. The same does not hold for the type of artworks that we will analyze in the next [two] sections, artworks in which the colors applied to the shapes represented *must be viewed as essential aspects of the shapes*. I will leave it to others to come up with a name for this genus of morphological artworks, because *morpho-chromatic artworks* is really much too awkward an expression.

32

We must first distinguish between two species of this genus of artwork according to the two ways of representing shape discussed above [i.e., plastic art versus graphic art or drawing]. The reader can apply the following discussion to the third way of representing shape discussed in §30 [e.g., reliefs, cameos, and coins].

Thus, let us first consider artworks that present the eye with shapes produced by bodies with the same shapes and that, moreover, have colors that we are supposed to view as essential to them. Here, too, we have to distinguish between two subtypes according to whether the shapes remain the same while we look at them or whether they change in some way while we look at them.

1. The *enduring works* of this type include:

   a. shapes that represent an *individual* or *group of people* as realistically as possible and are either made out of stone, wood, or another lifeless material that can be formed and colored to take on a humanlike appearance (sculpture) or composed of living people themselves, who remain as still as possible in a certain position and with certain gestures (*tableaux*);[20]

   b. *animal and plant shapes*, represented with various materials as realistically as possible;

   c. human, animal, or plant forms with miniature or enlarged proportions;

   d. buildings intended either as housing or for large assemblies, for religious, political, or scientific purposes, or for the pleasure of the community; these include public places decorated with columns and arcades, triumphal arches, and monuments to honored persons or memorable events;

   e. some furniture and utensils, such as vases, ovens, tables, chairs, and the like;

   f. landscape gardens, beautiful landscapes, and the like.

---

20. [*Tableaux*, including scenes reconstructed from paintings, were a popular entertainment in the nineteenth century.]

Everyone knows that guidance in how to create the listed objects in a beautiful way has already been drafted. However, it is debatable whether many of these objects should be recognized as genuine works of art. I will perhaps have occasion to express my own opinion on this matter at another time; at any rate, doing so here would lead us astray.

2. Objects *that change before the eyes of the spectator* include:

    a. representations of the various *human emotions*, as produced through mere gestures and movements of a real person who remains silent (mimicry);

    b. representations of *entire interactions* between multiple people, through mere gestures and movements, without speaking;

    c. marches (processions), dances, and the like;

    d. hunts, horsemanship, gymnastics, and much more;

    e. waterworks, fireworks, and much more.

33

The *second* species of *morpho-chromatic* art that we have to consider presents the imagination with shapes produced through the mere application of color to a surface, whereby the artist intends us to view the choice of color as an essential part of the artwork.

I will be permitted to call these artworks *paintings* and the art of creating them *the art of painting*.

But here, too, we must distinguish between *enduring* and *changing* artworks, between those that remain the same and those that change before our eyes.

1. In the first group, one justifiably differentiates between:

    a. the type of *object* represented in the painting, particularly:

        i. paintings of humans that are as realistic as possible (portraits),

        ii. paintings of animals, such as hunting scenes,

       iii.paintings of plants, such as flowers and fruits,

       iv. paintings of architecture,

       v. landscape painting, and much more;

   b. and the varieties of paint and their particular methods of application:

       i. watercolors,

       ii. pastels,

       iii.oil paintings,

       iv. encaustic painting,

       v. mosaics and the like.

2. Paintings that change before the eyes of the beholder include magic lanterns, phantasmagorias, anamorphic paintings, dioramas, Daguerre's and Janin's autoramas,[21] and the like. This class also includes paintings that—because they are not painted on an even surface, but on a surface that is broken or folded in some way—depict different objects depending on the spectator's viewpoint.

34

The only matter left for us to investigate now is what the above-discussed visual arts are capable of when they are combined with arts of mere thought, with sonic arts, or, finally, with both at the same time.

The arts of *pure thought* (it is easiest to begin with them once again) can be joined with the *visual* arts to pursue a common end, in ways that are similar to how they can be joined with the *sonic* arts [see

---

21. [The 1849 text has "Janues"; the 2021 edition has "Janin's." Bolzano appears to reference the entry on "Dioramas" in Hebenstreit's encyclopedia of aesthetics (see note 10), where the French writer and critic Jules Janin is mentioned as having described Louis Daguerre's 1822 diorama as the precursor of daguerreotype photography invented in 1839.]

§§25–27]—namely, *directly*, as well as through the *mediation of language* [i.e., indirectly].

1. The *direct* connection is by far the more important. It occurs whenever certain representations contained in a beautiful collection of thoughts need or deserve to be *illustrated* to us in a work of one of the visual arts—that is, when the artist produces an image of one of the objects subsumed under this representation. The visual arts can perform this service, which our sensibility not only welcomes but really cannot dispense with. And they can perform this service even when the artist who developed a beautiful collection of thoughts cannot articulate it in words or does not have a distinct grasp of it. What is more, there are representations that cannot be conveyed to us even in the clearest words, either because they cannot be reduced to simple concepts or because words have not yet succeeded in adequately articulating them. Examples include the representations of the *grace and dignity* that genuine wisdom and virtue bestow upon a person's mere *external appearance*, and representations embodied in the characteristic marks with which lust, pride, jealousy, and other vices brand us as their slaves. However, such representations can be taught to us by paintings much more quickly, less dangerously, and more pleasantly than could even the great teacher that we call *experience*.

2. Every artwork of mere thought has to be articulated in words in order to be fully communicated to others. But words disappear as soon as they are uttered, no matter how beautiful the utterance might be; indeed, they disappear even if they are delivered to our ears with the assistance of all of the sonic arts. As a consequence, they can only be heard by a few people and even these few quickly forget them. Hence it is clear that the preservation of such an artwork can only be *secured* for the future when the *collection of words* that captures the *collection of thoughts* in question is first *written down* or, even better, when it is reproduced in *print*. This turns the artwork of mere thought into an object that can be perceived *by the eye*, and thus, *visual* arts can join with it. Nobody who has ever encountered a successful artwork of mere thought and believed that reproducing it would not only please but also contribute to the development and morality of humanity could be blamed for wanting what was so beautifully said to be beautifully represented *in writing*. The aid that the visual arts in this way render to

an artwork of thought constitutes the *indirect* joining of the two arts. The visual arts perform a merely external service for the artwork of thought, a service that consists wholly in the fact that people are more inclined to read a book when it has a beautiful appearance.

Let us now consider in more detail the new artworks that come into being in both ways [i.e., directly and indirectly].

35

The discussion up to now is sufficient to show that the visual arts can hardly accomplish anything greater than when they support an artwork of thought in the direct mode discussed in point (1) of the previous section. After all, can there be anything more important than contributing to the development of our most noble sensibilities, such as our moral and religious feelings, in a way that can be grasped even by the simplest person [*roheste Mensch*], even by a child? Do I have to tell anyone that even such a person enjoys looking at images and statues and often loses themselves for hours in looking at them, thinking about their meaning, and trying to decipher what they are trying to say? And especially when we offer even just a little help by giving them an easily communicated explanation, which they will listen to gratefully? In this context, it should not be forgotten that not only one, but almost all the types of artworks of mere thought listed in §15 can be helpfully supplemented by the visual arts. After all, high-quality images, paintings, plastic works, phantoms, and the like cannot only facilitate but are sometimes even indispensable for many arts and sciences, including the description of nature, natural science, geography, ethnography, the history of humanity, anatomy and physiology, and nosology. But although the service that the visual arts render these arts and sciences is often of high importance, it is only seldom true that performing the service increases the value of visual artworks themselves. What I mean is that the value of images as artworks is not necessarily increased by their performing this service; indeed, as mentioned above, it is disputed whether even the most successful illustrations deserve to be called genuine works of art. But I do not mean this comment to apply to cases when *literary art* is combined with a visual art, and certainly not when this is done with the intention of bringing certain moral or religious ideals to light.

What I stated at the beginning of this section only applies to artworks created with this very intention. Art only produces its *highest*, its truly immortal, *masterpieces* with the assistance of this intention, which is really assistance from God. Or at least, it can only seek to produce such great works with this assistance. I would like to add only that the amount of material that morality and religion—and particularly the Christian religion, indeed, the Catholic-Christian religion— provides for artistic rendering is truly inexhaustible.

But when are we permitted to say that a visual artwork is *inventive*? My answer is: only when the artist does not represent the object with which he wants to occupy our attention exactly how it might appear in reality. Rather, a visual artwork is inventive when the artist gives the represented object certain qualities that are not intended to be taken as actual qualities of the object but that serve the purpose of inciting in us certain feelings, sensations, wishes, and resolutions of the will that we transfer onto the represented object. In other words, a visual work of art is *inventive*, or at least contains *inventive elements*, if, upon viewing it, the representation *first evoked* in us (what we see) adds to the object that the work *actually represents* qualities that the object does not actually have, and that we do not attribute to it in reality (if we are not to misunderstand the artist's intention). We only use its representing the object as having those qualities in order to evoke particular feelings, sensations, wishes, and resolutions of the will.

Such works include:

1. *All works depicting historical scenes* (whether they consist in single statues, groups of statues, paintings, or mere drawings), so long as they contain elements not rooted in historical fact but added by the artist, such as the color and drape of clothing, the staffage,[22] and the like. Moreover, such representations always require an *inscription* that identifies the object in cases where it is not readily recognizable through certain unmistakable attributes or certain generally established forms. At any rate, it is

---

22. [Staffage is the depiction of human or animal figures as background in a scene.]

well known that the art of creating beautiful historical—and in particular *political-historical*—paintings has long constituted its own genre of art, which is called *history painting*.

2. *Images intended to illustrate a fable*, where it would be pointless and indeed inappropriate were the representations of humans and animals totally realistic, because everything should be tailored through poetry to fit the image's purpose, namely, the *moral* of the fable.

An *inscription* that identifies the represented fable or, if it is not sufficiently well known, retells the fable itself is even more indispensable here.

3. By contrast, that *symbolic and allegorical artworks* do not need anything further to identify the objects they represent is seen as one of their perfections.

4. *Representations of ideals* that are inventive to a high degree—that is, representations of a sensory object that communicate a *principle* as perfectly as a visual art is capable of doing.

5. All somewhat *embellished representations of real objects* that, without destroying the similarity altogether, leave out some disfigurations or add some beauty that is lacking—for example, portraits.

6. *Caricatures*—that is, representations that, in contrast to embellished representations, magnify a person's ugliness, and in particular the ugliness that is a consequence of the person's moral failings, in order to increase our revulsion toward those failings. Other types of disfiguration that do not aim to and cannot evoke such a moral effect are not, for this very reason, justified and thus have no place in a genuine work of art.

7. All so-called *didactic works*, which, because every work of art has to have some kind of bias or intention, are only distinguished from other artworks by the fact that their purpose is particularly important for their creation, and is more openly displayed.

8. *Genre paintings*, so long as the artist is capable of expressing an inventive thought through these common and apparently lowly objects.

9. Finally, the lowest type of artworks, which can hardly be counted among inventive works of art, are arabesques and similar products of visual art that pursue no other end than perhaps to surprise us with their fantastic compositions of pure imagination. Nevertheless, consideration is due to *Hegel's* proposal that we treat such arabesques as *symbolic of the transitions between the three realms of nature,*[23] in which case they would be inventive. Should it not now be possible to expand on this proposal?

36

I have little to say about the *second* [indirect] mode of combining the arts of thought with the visual arts: the art of beautifully presenting in writing (or print) beautiful thoughts composed in beautiful words (§34). At any rate, calligraphy (of which the art of book printing has doubtless been a species since its invention) has always been counted among the fine arts, and sometimes one expends perhaps too many resources on some works for their beautiful typography and decoration. Thus, it seems that the importance of this art has not been forgotten. What is lamentable is only that there seems to be too little recognition of—or at least too little willingness to pay attention to—the three requirements for beautiful writing: first, the simplicity of its signs, second, the ease of distinguishing between them, and, third, their pleasing shape.

37

Up to this point (§§33–36), we have only considered combinations of the arts of thought and the visual arts that present to the eye something enduring. But there are also such artworks *that change before the eyes of the recipient.* This kind of artwork is produced when one of the types of

---

23. [Hegel 1975: 658.]

visual artwork referenced in points (2) of §§32 and 33, which consist of *appearances that alter over time*, is combined with something *inventive*. In effect, visual artworks that change over time ultimately consist in a bunch of distinct artworks that, for their part, do not change for a very brief period of time or do not have to change. Moreover, in §35, we observed that this latter type of artwork is often combined with arts of thought and sometimes even with inventiveness, which is always done with the exclusive aim of increasing the visual artwork's value. Both of these considerations taken together leave no doubt that, among the visual artworks that change over time, there might be—indeed, there are—some that contain more or less inventiveness, or may be combined with yet another art of thought. The more energy an artist has to exert in producing visual artworks like these, the more he must seek to increase their value with the powerful help of inventiveness, in order to gain assurance that the work garners the desired praise. And would not the changes in the artworks themselves prompt him to inventive thoughts that could be used in the work of art?

38

The connection between the visual arts and the sonic arts is not nearly as immediate and close as are the visual arts' connections with the arts of mere thought, especially literary art. After all, in order for a sonic art and a visual art to be combined in some work, it is clearly not enough for both simply to affect our senses simultaneously—for music to fill our ears while we are looking at a painting. Rather, the effect produced by one of these arts must be augmented and perfected by the effect of the other. Only then can one speak of a complex work of art composed of the products of both arts. There is no question that combining the two arts for a common end is possible. Visual artworks that change before the recipient's eyes are particularly well suited to be joined with an art whose products are so fleeting that they can never be fixed. When children and young people hear cheerful music, do they not feel almost compelled to make a dancing movement and thus to create a visual work of art that changes as we watch? In this case, the musical artwork calls forth the visual artwork without further effort. Similarly, in other cases, the mere sight of a rhythmic movement will spur our imagination to think up some music. And when we see something change before our eyes that does not have any recognizable rhythm, we will perhaps not require but will still welcome accompanying music, if the sensations that it evokes in us harmonize with those evoked by the scene we are witnessing.

Strictly speaking, if the two arts of the external senses are to work together without a third art, namely, literary art, being added to the mix, then neither what the eye sees nor what the ear hears can have an *inventive* component. In accordance with the reasoning so far, this means that the colors and shapes that we see and the sounds and sequences that we hear cannot prompt our imagination to develop certain *thoughts* (representations and propositions), which, although we do not necessarily attribute any truth value to them, nevertheless evoke in us sensations, wishes, and resolutions of the will in a way that we recognize as having been intended by the artist. It is obvious that this absence of inventive content cannot be seen as a merit of an artwork. Rather, it seems justified to desire that literary art make its contribution to the greater perfection of artworks that combine the visual and musical arts, a contribution that is so simple to add and, if it is done correctly, always adds value. But then the resulting work of art would no longer comprise just *two* arts; it will comprise *three* arts, the category that we will consider in the next section.

39

The genre of artworks that will conclude this essay is composed of all three main types of art. To honor human ingenuity, we should remark that even the most ancient times and the least developed peoples [*rohesten Völkern*] brought forth artworks of this type, such as dances with song and instrumental music. These are works of fine art, even though they might be very imperfect, might do nothing for our more developed tastes, and might even be degenerately abused to encourage and satisfy ignominious desires. Yet although we have made much progress for the better (which would not have been possible without the beneficent influence of Christianity), we should not for a moment convince ourselves that our taste is perfect, that we have already discovered all possible arts that could be produced by combining one or more arts of mere thought with the visual or musical arts, or that our artworks have reached the apex of perfection possible for humans. As far as technical proficiency and everything that creates powerful sensations is concerned, we have made incredible advances—in any case, we have achieved in this respect much more than genuine taste can judge to be beautiful. As for where we continue to fall short, we are still so retrograde that only a small number of our artists really know what their mission is.

For now, the most important artistic accomplishments of this genus that have become common among us are, roughly speaking, the following:

1. *holding a speech*, which occurs at such important occasions and under such circumstances that we may reasonably expect that the speaker will have carefully selected all his words as well as his entire comportment and even his clothing;

2. reciting a *poem*;

3. a *prayer*, publicly spoken or even *sung* in a house of worship under conditions similar to those stated in (1), with or without organ accompaniment, and the like;

4. *plastic* or *graphic representations*, whether they be static or change before the recipient's eyes, that are augmented by music or *song* that supplements their effect;

5. *parades of people* that create a stimulating or calming sight through their intentional comportment, certain symbols (flags, torches, etc.), and even their *clothing*, a sight that is then bolstered through fitting music or *songs*;

6. such parades that are performed in a space with such qualities that it contributes to the intended moral or religious purpose, such as a purposively decorated church, a graveyard, the free temple of nature, or a place that reveals to us God's great blessings, and so forth;

7. *dances* with music, ballets, allegorical dances, historical dances, and the like;

8. *theatrical plays* that are not merely read, but (as one says) *performed.*

In the artworks listed in (1), (2), and (3), the artist's person itself contributes to the effect of the artwork. He uses his own body and gestures to bring forth the visual component of the artwork, and he uses his voice to bring forth its sonic component. The blunders committed by so many people amply demonstrate the need for lessons in these arts, so that the speaker does everything in the right way, expressively, without seeming overdone. And nobody will dispute that the actor's work is even more difficult. Finally, some manifestations of artworks that have to be performed by multiple people will be pretty insignificant, or at any rate, the task demanded of individuals will be pretty easy, so that no particular guidance is needed. However, for artworks in which every part is thought through and organized in detail, guidance and a special theory become all the more necessary the greater the degree of complexity and the number of arts involved. Since there are really no limits for this type of art, it is understandable that there is no way to determine the number of theories of complex arts that will be needed and thus that might be articulated over time, as humanity progresses.

LIST OF EXPLICATIONS

The **beautiful** must be an object whose contemplation can cause pleasure in all people whose cognitive powers are duly developed. This pleasure occurs because, after apprehending some of the object's qualities, the formation of a concept of the object is neither too easy nor too difficult and does not occasion the rigor of distinct thought. Moreover, the pleasure occurs because the concept thus formed, in making it possible to guess at those qualities of the object only accessible to further contemplation, affords at least an obscure awareness of the proficiency of one's cognitive powers. (CB §11)

We understand **aesthetics** to be a scientifically organized collection of all those truths worth knowing that satisfy either one of the two following conditions: They are truths that immediately concern the beautiful. Alternatively, they are truths that stand in such a relation to the beautiful that at least one—the truths that immediately concern the beautiful or those that stand in relation to the beautiful—must be properly understood and fruitfully applied in light of the other. (CFA §1)

We say that a person possesses beautiful artistry, or (what is the same) we call him an **artist**, when he has the ability to produce, through his free and intentional acts, objects subsumed under the concept of the beautiful in such a way that their beautiful qualities are the result of his technique, which is, in the production of the object, oriented toward this end [of making objects beautiful] and which is thereby conducted in one way and not in any other. We call these objects themselves (more or less perfect) works of fine art or **artworks**. (CFA §2)

Guidance on the beautiful will only be warranted when we are dealing with the production of an object that we can allow ourselves time to reflect on and that we seek to preserve and make communicable to others, such that it is reasonable to expect that many people will sooner or later observe it with pleasure and benefit, which will be augmented in proportion to the number of beautiful qualities that we have given it. (CFA §5)

We may view as belonging to a **single art** only those practices whose parts cannot, for reason of their nature, be split up or distributed among multiple individuals for execution and, moreover, whose teaching requires a continuous course of study, as the one part cannot be understood or applied without the other. (CFA §6)

I call a work of art complex and the art of which it is an instance a **complex art** only when the production of the work of art requires practices that are, in general, carried out by different individuals or at least stand in such a loose relationship to one another that it is most practical to teach them separately. (CFA §6)

REFERENCES

Abrams, M. H. 1989. "Art-as-Such: The Sociology of Modern Aesthetics," *Bulletin of the American Academy of Arts and Sciences* 38.6: 8–33.

Addison, Joseph. 1711. *The Spectator* 29 (April 3).

Aristotle. 1987. *The Poetics of Aristotle*, trans. Stephen Halliwell. Chapel Hill: University of North Carolina Press.

———. 2018. *Rhetoric*, trans. C. D. C. Reeve. Cambridge, MA: Hackett.

Baumgartner, Wilhelm, and Lynn Pasquerella. 2006. "Brentano's Value Theory: Beauty, Goodness, and the Concept of Correct Emotion," *Cambridge Companion to Brentano*, ed. Dale Jacquette. Cambridge: Cambridge University Press.

Bolzano, Bernard. 2004. *The Mathematical Works of Bernard Bolzano*, ed. and trans. Steve Russ. Oxford: Oxford University Press.

———. 2007. *Selected Writings on Ethics and Politics*, ed. and trans. Paul Rusnock and Rolf George. Amsterdam: Rodopi.

———. 2014[1837]. *Theory of Science*, ed. and trans. Paul Rusnock and Rolf George, 4 vols. Oxford: Oxford University Press.

———. 2017. *Écrits Esthétiques de Bernard Bolzano*, ed. and trans. Carole Maigné, Jan Šebestík, and Nicolas Rialland. Paris: Vrin.

———. 2021. *Gesamtausgabe, Nachlaß: Ästhetische Schriften*, series II, vol. 13, ed. Jan Berg, Edgar Morscher, and Peter Michael Schenkel. Stuttgart: Frommann-Holzboog.

Buchenau, Stefanie. 2021. "A Modern Diotima: Johanna Charlotte Unzer Between Wolffianism, Aestheticism, and Popular Philosophy," *Women and Philosophy in Eighteenth-Century Germany*, ed. Corey W. Dyck. Oxford: Oxford University Press.

Carnap, Rudolf. 1947. *Meaning and Necessity: A Study in Semantics and Modal Logic*. Chicago: University of Chicago Press.

Copenhaver, Rebecca. 2015. "Thomas Reid on Aesthetic Perception," *Thomas Reid on Mind, Knowledge, and Value*, ed. Rebecca Copenhaver and Todd Buras. Oxford: Oxford University Press.

Dummett, Michael. 1991. *Frege and Other Philosophers*. Oxford: Oxford University Press.

Franssen, Maarten. 1991. "The Ocular Harpsichord of Louis-Bertrand Castel: The Science and Aesthetics of an Eighteenth-Century Cause Célèbre," *Tractrix* 3: 15–77.

Gerhardus, Dietfried. 1972. "Bolzanos methodische Grundlegung einer rezeptionstheoretisch aufgebauten Ästhetik," *Untersuchungen zur Grundlegung der Ästhetik*. Frankfurt: Athenäum Verlag.

Guyer, Paul. 2014. *A History of Modern Aesthetics*. 3 vols. Cambridge: Cambridge University Press.

Halliwell, Stephen. 2002. *The Aesthetics of Mimesis: Ancient Texts and Modern Problems*. Princeton: Princeton University Press.

Hegel, Georg Wilhelm Friedrich. 1975. *Aesthetics: Lectures on Fine Art*, trans. T. M. Knox. Oxford: Oxford University Press.

———. 2010. *The Science of Logic*, ed. and trans. George di Giovanni. Cambridge: Cambridge University Press.

Hopkins, Robert. 1998. *Picture, Image, and Experience: A Philosophical Inquiry*. Cambridge: Cambridge University Press.

Kant, Immanuel. 2000[1790]. *Critique of the Power of Judgement*, ed. Paul Guyer, trans. Paul Guyer and Eric Matthews. Cambridge: Cambridge University Press.

Kelley, Michael, ed. 2014. *Oxford Encyclopedia of Aesthetics*, 2nd ed., 4 vols. Oxford: Oxford University Press.

Kivy, Peter. 2012. "What Really Happened in the Eighteenth Century: The 'Modern System' Re-examined (Again)," *British Journal of Aesthetics* 52.1: 61–74.

Krämer, Stephan. 2011. "Bolzano on the Intransparency of Content," *Grazer Philosophische Studien* 82.1: 189–208.

Kristeller, P. O. 1951–52. "The Modern System of the Arts," *Journal of the History of Ideas* 12.4: 496–527 and 13.1: 17–46.

Lapointe, Sandra. 2011. *Bolzano's Theoretical Philosophy*. London: Palgrave Macmillan.

Lena, Jennifer C. 2019. *Entitled: Discriminating Tastes and the Expansion of the Arts*. Princeton: Princeton University Press.

Livingston, Paisley. 2014. "Bolzano on Beauty," *British Journal of Aesthetics* 54.3: 269–84.

———. 2015. "An Introduction to Bolzano's Essay on Beauty," *Estetika: The European Journal of Aesthetics* 52.2: 203–28.

———. 2016. "Bolzano on Art," *British Journal of Aesthetics* 56.4: 333–45.

———. 2022. "Review of Bernard Bolzano, *Gesamtausgabe, Nachlaß: Ästhetische Schriften*," *British Journal of Aesthetics*. Forthcoming.

Lopes, Dominic McIver. 2014. *Beyond Art*. Oxford: Oxford University Press.

———. 2019. "Feeling for Freedom: K. C. Bhattacharyya on *Rasa*," *British Journal of Aesthetics* 59.4: 465–77.

———. 2022. "Beautiful Philosophy," *Bloomsbury Contemporary Aesthetics*, ed. Darren Hudson Hick. London: Bloomsbury.

Maigné, Carole. 2017. "Introduction," *Écrits Esthétiques de Bernard Bolzano*, ed. and trans. Carole Maigné, Jan Šebestík, and Nicolas Rialland. Paris: Vrin.

Matherne, Samantha. 2020. "Edith Landmann-Kalischer on Aesthetic Demarcation and Normativity," *British Journal of Aesthetics* 60.3: 315–34.

Matthen, Mohan. 2020. "Art Forms Emerging: An Approach to Evaluative Diversity in Art," *Journal of Aesthetics and Art Criticism* 78.3: 303–18.

McCormick, Peter. 1981. "Bolzano and the Dark Doctrine: An Essay in Aesthetics," *Structure and Gestalt: Philosophy and Literature in Austria-Hungary and Her Successor States*, ed. Barry Smith. Amsterdam: Benjamins.

Morscher, Edgar. 2018. "Bernard Bolzano," *Stanford Encyclopedia of Philosophy*, ed. Edward N. Zalta. <https://plato.stanford.edu/entries/bolzano>.

Porter, James I. 2009. "Is Art Modern? Kristeller's 'Modern System of the Arts' Reconsidered," *British Journal of Aesthetics* 49.1: 1–24.

Příhonský, František. 2014[1850]. *New Anti-Kant*, ed. and trans. Sandra Lapointe and Clinton Tolley. London: Palgrave Macmillan.

Reber, Rolf, Norbert Schwarz, and Piotr Winkielman. 2004. "Processing Fluency and Aesthetic Pleasure: Is Beauty in the Perceiver's Processing Experience?" *Personality and Social Psychology Review* 8.4: 364–82.

Reicher, Maria E. 2006. "Austrian Aesthetics," *The Austrian Contribution to Analytic Philosophy*, ed. Mark Textor. London: Routledge.

Rusnock, Paul, and Jan Šebestík. 2019. *Bolzano, His Life and Work*. Oxford: Oxford University Press.

Schaeffer, Jean-Marie. 2000. *Art of the Modern Age: Philosophy of Art from Kant to Heidegger*, trans. Steven Rendall. Princeton: Princeton University Press.

Shiner, Larry. 2001. *The Invention of Art: A Cultural History*. Chicago: University of Chicago Press.

Whiting, Daniel. 2022. "Cavendish's Aesthetic Realism," *Philosopher's Imprint*. Forthcoming.

Vesper, Achim. 2012. "Contempler, Distinguer: Bolzano sur la Conceptualité de la Perception Esthétique," *Esthétique et Logique*, ed. Charlotte Morel. Villeneuve d'Ascq: Presses Universitaires du Septentrion.

Wolterstorff, Nicholas. 2015. *Art Rethought: The Social Practices of Art*. Oxford: Oxford University Press.

Young, James O. 2015. "The Ancient and Modern System of the Arts," *British Journal of Aesthetics* 55.1: 1–17.

Zuckert, Rachel. 2019. *Herder's Naturalist Aesthetics*. Cambridge: Cambridge University Press.

Index

Abrams, M. H., 2, 5–6, 17–18
Addison, Joseph, 6, 17
Adorno, Theodor, xxv
aesthetic ideas, 27–28, 31
aesthetics: and history in, 83;
  nature of, 82; philosophy of
  science, 15–17, 21, 42, 77, 82.
  See also beauty
allegory, 126
Aristotle, 96
arts: absolute, 94; construction
  and consumption models of,
  5–6, 17–18; institutions, 7;
  nature of, 1–8, 19, 32–33,
  82–83, 85, 89–91; as practical,
  22, 93–94; revisionism about,
  20–21, 31–32; simple versus
  complex, 22, 90–92. *See also*
  arts of thought; creativity;
  mixed arts; oratory; performance; poetry; sonic arts;
  visual arts
arts of thought, 96–102; commu-
  nication of, 101–2; language
  in, 100–101; representations,
  97–98; in teaching, 100–101;
  truths, 99–100
association, laws of, 110
Austrian Empire, xii
awareness, xx–xxi, 8–11, 13, 59,
  62, 65, 71

beauty: in the arts, 7, 17–21,
  81–82, 86; and charming, 44;
  and cognitive development,
  12–13, 48–49, 53, 69; distinctively human, 12–13, 50–51,
  56; diversity of, 8, 12–13,
  48–50, 79–80; immediacy
  of, 68; moral, 30, 66, 69–70;
  nonartistic, 7, 12, 18; objects
  of, 72–76, 89, 94, 97–98, 105;
  pleasure in, 43–45, 55–59;
  response-dependence of, 13;
  revisionism of, 14, 16–17,
  65–67; rule-based, 5, 75–77,
  67, 119; simple, 72–74; and
  utility, 45, 55–56, 58–59, 66,
  69–70, 87; versus good, 42–43
Bronn, Wilhelm, 83, 88–89
caricature, 126
Carnap, Rudolf, 14
Castel, Louis Bertrand, 115–16
Chambers, Ephraim, 2–3
charming, 44
clear and distinct. *See* concepts:
  obscure
concepts, 2, 8–11, 26–27; coextensive, 15, 39, 41, 63–65;
  explication of, 14–16, 36;
  formation of, xxiv, 29, 56,
  79–80; introspection of,
  15–16, 41–42; obscure, xxi,